# TO THE READER

This book is presented in its original form and is part of the
religious literature and works of Scientology® Founder, L. Ron
Hubbard. It is a record of Mr. Hubbard's observations and research
into the nature of man and each individual's capabilities as a
spiritual being, and is not a statement of claims made by the author,
publisher or any Church of Scientology.

Scientology is defined as the study and handling of the spirit in
relationship to itself, universes and other life. Thus, the mission of
the Church of Scientology is a simple one: to help the individual
regain his true nature, as a spiritual being, and thereby attain an
awareness of his relationship with his fellow man and the universe.
Therein lies the path to personal integrity, trust, enlightenment,
and spiritual freedom itself.

Scientology and its forerunner and substudy, Dianetics, as
practiced by the Church, address only the "thetan" (spirit), which
is senior to the body, and its relationship to and effects on the body.
While the Church is free, as all churches are, to engage in spiritual
healing, its primary goal is increased spiritual awareness for all.
For this reason, neither Scientology nor Dianetics is offered as, nor
professes to be physical healing, nor is any claim made to that effect.
The Church does not accept individuals who desire treatment of
physical or mental illness but, instead, requires a competent medical
examination for physical conditions, by qualified specialists, before
addressing their spiritual cause.

The Hubbard® Electrometer, or E-Meter, is a religious artifact
used in the Church. The E-Meter, by itself, does nothing and is only
used by ministers and ministers-in-training, qualified in its use, to
help parishioners locate the source of spiritual travail.

The attainment of the benefits and goals of the Scientology
religion requires each individual's dedicated participation, as only
through one's own efforts can they be achieved.

We hope reading this book is only one step of a personal voyage
of discovery into this new and vital world religion.

## THIS BOOK BELONGS TO

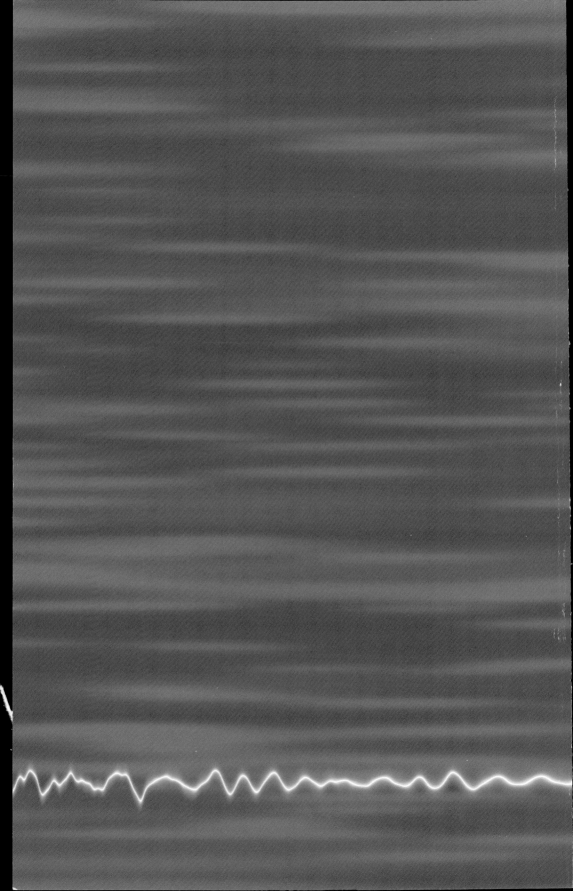

# SCIENTOLOGY 8-80

# SCIENTOLOGY 8-80

## THE DISCOVERY AND INCREASE OF LIFE ENERGY IN THE GENUS HOMO SAPIENS

$$Life = \frac{EI}{-R} \cdot (-f)$$

*If:*

    E  = Energy Potential

    I  = Energy Flow

    –R = Negative Resistance

    –f = Negative Frequency

# L. RON HUBBARD

Bridge
Publications, Inc.

A
HUBBARD®
PUBLICATION

*Published by*
BRIDGE PUBLICATIONS, INC.
4751 Fountain Avenue
Los Angeles, California 90029

ISBN 978-1-4031-4415-7

# IMPORTANT NOTE

In reading this book, be very certain you never go past a word you do not fully understand. The only reason a person gives up a study or becomes confused or unable to learn is because he or she has gone past a word that was not understood.

The confusion or inability to grasp or learn comes AFTER a word the person did not have defined and understood. It may not only be the new and unusual words you have to look up. Some commonly used words can often be misdefined and so cause confusion.

This datum about not going past an undefined word is the most important fact in the whole subject of study. Every subject you have taken up and abandoned had its words which you failed to get defined.

Therefore, in studying this book be very, very certain you never go past a word you do not fully understand. If the material becomes confusing or you can't seem to grasp it, there will be a word just earlier that you have not understood. Don't go any further, but go back to BEFORE you got into trouble, find the misunderstood word and get it defined.

## GLOSSARY

To aid reader comprehension, L. Ron Hubbard directed the editors to provide a glossary. This is included in the Appendix, *Editor's Glossary of Words, Terms and Phrases*. Words sometimes have several meanings. The *Editor's Glossary* only contains the definitions of words as they are used in this text. Other definitions can be found in standard language or Dianetics and Scientology dictionaries.

If you find any other words you do not know, look them up in a good dictionary.

# CONTENTS

## Part One
### July 1952

# Part Two
### August 1952

# Part Three
### September 1952

#  P A R T

"The goal of the auditor is to rehabilitate
the self-determinism of his preclear,
to bring back his hope and power,

# ONE

*July 1952*

*to get his preclear up to where the preclear,*
*all of his own, knows."*

# CHAPTER ONE

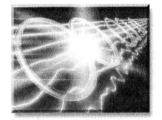

# THE AUDITOR'S CODE

# THE AUDITOR'S CODE

**Y**OU CAN FIND the Auditor's Code elsewhere. It is enough, here, to say that an auditor is one who clears away the errors of his fellows and that a good auditor, in doing so, does not lay further error in.

The goal of the auditor is to rehabilitate the self-determinism of his preclear, to bring back his hope and power, to get his preclear up to where the preclear, all of his own, *KNOWS*.

The preclear has to take very little on faith with these techniques. He simply runs what he is told.

The auditor should not bully his preclear or evaluate for him.

Most important, the auditor should choose for his preclear a person worth salvaging, who will in his turn help another.

We have so much to do!

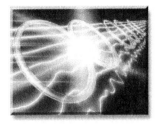

# LIFE AS A MIRROR

# LIFE AS A MIRROR

IFE IS A STATIC, according to the Axioms. A static has no motion. It has no wavelength. The proofs and details of this are elsewhere in Scientology.

This static has the peculiarity of acting as a "mirror." It records and holds the images of motion. It can even create motion and record and hold the image of that. It records, also, space and time in order to record motion which is, after all, only "change in space through time." Played against motion, as a kinetic, the static can produce live energy.

In a mind, any mind, the basic beingness is found to be a static which can create motion and on which motion can be recorded and which, acting against motion, produces energy.

A memory is a recording of the physical universe. It contains, any memory, a *time* index (when it happened) and a pattern of motion. Like a lake reflects the trees and moving clouds, so does a memory reflect the physical universe. Sight, sound, pain, emotion, effort, conclusions and many other things are recorded in this static for any given instant of observation.

Such a memory we call a "facsimile." The mind, examining a facsimile it has made, can see it, feel it, hear it, re-experience the pain in it, the effort, the emotion.

There are billions of facsimiles available to any mind. Billions of billions. These facsimiles can be brought into present time by the environment and, "unseen" or "unknown" by the awareness of awareness of the mind, can re-impress their pains, efforts and aberrations upon the being, thus making one less liable to survive. All unknowingnesses, confusions, aberrations, psychosomatic ills are traceable to facsimiles.

One believes he can use *any* facsimile he has ever received. He has been hurt. He uses the facsimile of being hurt to hurt another.

But as one Survives as well as everything else survives, to hurt another is *wrong*. One *regrets* the injury, seeking to turn back time (which *is* regret). Thus the facsimile he used becomes interlocked with his facsimile of trying to use it and both facsimiles "hang up" and travel with present time. One even gets the *pain* he seeks to inflict on another, this being the action against him of the facsimile he sought to give, by action, to another. It startles the preclear, when run through a boyhood fight wherein he hit another boy in the eye, to feel the pain in his *own* eye at the instant of the blow. And so it is with *all* inflicted injuries.

This is a simple matter of the interaction of the pictures of energy.

This is a "maybe," indecision, inaction. This is aberration–trying to do unto others what was done to you–good or bad.

An interplay of static against motion or between two classes of motion, one relatively static to the other, can and does produce active electrical energy in beings of different characteristics and potentials. This makes a living being an electrical field more capable of high potential and varieties of waves than are known to nuclear physics, of which Scientology is a basic.

This created energy, played lightly over a facsimile, reactivates it and causes it to bear upon a being once more. This is an activity of thinking.

A facsimile brought into play by a moment of intense activity may afterwards, when the being is again producing only normal energy output, "refuse" to be handled by the lower energy. This facsimile then can trap the energy of a being and turn upon him the pain, emotion and other things recorded in the facsimile. The facsimile thus can absorb energy and give pain, especially when the being holding it has forgotten it or does not perceive it. This is "restimulation."

By concentrating a live energy flow upon a facsimile directly, the being can erase, disintegrate, or "explode" or "implode" it.

As heavy facsimiles are the hidden source of human aberration and psychosomatic illness, their erasure or better handling by the being is intensely desirable.

The remedy of human aberration and illness is a minor goal of Scientology. Its discoveries make this possible.

# CHAPTER THREE

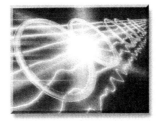

# FACSIMILES

# FACSIMILES

I F LIFE–OR THETA ($\theta$) as it is called in Scientology–is a mirror and a creator of motion which can be mirrored, it follows then that, mirror-wise, the whole of the laws of motion, magnetism, energy, matter and space and time can be found in *thought*–and behavior and even thinking partake of the physical universe laws regarding matter, energy, space and time. Thus even the laws of Newton can be found operative in thought. Fortunately, all this is beyond the need of an auditor's immediate grasp of the subject. For if it were not, an auditor would have to be first a nuclear physicist before he could begin to make the lame well and the able more able. Some understanding of the matter is, however, desirable–otherwise some very weird philosophies will develop which will benefit none. And Man has been ridden to death by philosophies which, unproven by any result, yet achieved enough prominence to spoil many a society (Schopenhauer or Nietzsche for example). And many a scientific effort has fallen into disrepute because of philosophic misrepresentation. Kant and Hegel all but ruined any hope nuclear physics or the humanities had by wild misinterpretation (in resounding language) of Indian philosophy and other early efforts to resolve the riddle of existence. So let us see how very basic and simple are the reasons *why* we audit *what* we audit.

Life can create motion or use motion or mirror motion. Motion is a change in space. Any change involves time. Conversely, for there to be time, there must be change. If no change occurs we have the illusion of a static again.

The main trouble with facsimiles is that they "hang up" in time, then become timeless and then give the concept of "no change." Our preclear, desiring to change for the better, cannot change because he is "hung up" in a memory which he "can't" change. The auditor wants change. Timelessness or foreverness prevents change and these unwelcome conditions come about when a facsimile "hangs up" in present time. This makes the preclear feel he is unable to change. No matter what you do for him, if you do not get him "into present time" or (the same thing) get the facsimiles out of present time, you have "no change."

Thus we had better know what makes a facsimile "hang up" and, "hung up," act upon the preclear.

We see that a facsimile is a mirror of old motions. It is undone and gotten out of present time by dropping out its "motion."

Only the mind can put the "motion" of a facsimile back into motion in the physical universe.

The facsimile is "made" by the mind's ability to duplicate the wave or motion patterns of the physical universe.

A "live" attention unit operates only in present time. A facsimile is composed of "dead" attention units, a pattern once made by "live" units in some past present time. For example, one sees a man. His attention units could be said, in that instant, to make up the pattern of what he sees. A moment later he has a facsimile made up of "dead" attention units. He can "see" this man again simply by throwing *live* units at patterns of *dead* units.

The facsimile can come "alive" and active only when scanned by live units. Then it can stay "alive" so long as live units are fixed on it. It will not "run out" or dissipate unless a large number of live units are played on it. Thus a facsimile can "hang up." This is an analogy, but it will do for an auditor.

An auditor can "see" his preclear as a mind which is surrounded by old facsimiles which are given just enough attention to keep them "in present time." It is the task of the auditor to drop *all* facsimiles into an inactive state. It is a grim fact that one really doesn't think with these heavy facsimiles. *One could survive quite well if he had no facsimiles!* Thought can pervade an area or approximate a situation and *know.* It thinks, the mind, with light facsimiles or no facsimiles at all.

Thus there is a compulsion early on the track to have facsimiles. Then as one ceases to "know," one is at length no longer in control of his facsimiles but is *their* victim. Given enough facsimiles a man dies, a theta being decays until it can't even be a man.

How, then, does one strip away facsimiles from the present time of the preclear? The auditor would have to audit billions of them to erase all the facsimiles the preclear has made or "borrowed" and which now act heavily upon him, giving him illness, degradation and aberration as well as amnesia as to his actual past.

We can rehabilitate the preclear by raising his ability to create energy and thus bring him to a "speed" which has sufficient output for him to overcome facsimiles. We do this by erasing or reducing certain facsimiles and, in doing so, retrain our preclear to produce a higher energy potential.

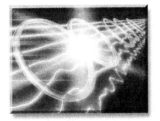

# WAVELENGTHS

# $\mathcal{W}$AVELENGTHS

WAVELENGTH IS a characteristic of motion. Many motions are too random, too chaotic to have orderly wavelengths. An orderly wavelength is a flow of motion. It has a regular repeated distance between its crests. Take a rope or the garden hose and give it a flip. You will see a wave travel along it. Energy–whether electrical, light or sound–has some such pattern.

Wavelength

This is a smooth flowing wave. Its length is between crests. It is measured in units of length, such as centimeters or inches or feet.

A flow can have many patterns.

These still have wavelength. We are not here much interested in *patterns* or *characteristics.* We are interested in *lengths.*

Here are some rough estimates of wavelengths which produce reactions on the mind, a Tone Scale of Wavelengths. (Accurate lengths not given here.)

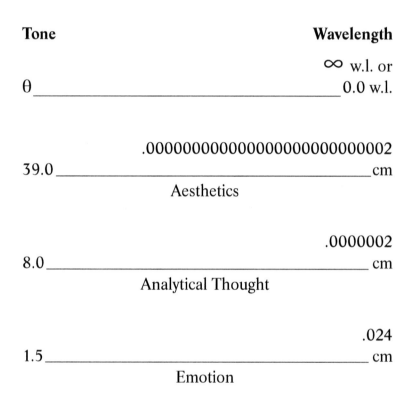

| Tone | Wavelength |
|------|-----------|
| θ | ∞ w.l. or 0.0 w.l. |
| 39.0 | .000000000000000000000000002 cm |
| | Aesthetics |
| 8.0 | .0000002 cm |
| | Analytical Thought |
| 1.5 | .024 cm |
| | Emotion |

Note how gross is emotion, how tiny is the wave producing aesthetics (art).

A wavelength is not the *power* of a wave. A small length, given enough volume, is deadlier or stronger than a gross wave.

Now we see that a facsimile can have a mirrored set of wavelengths which match any wave in the physical universe. Actually theta can create waves. Thus a facsimile can contain heavy effort or emotion and throw that back at the preclear.

# CHAPTER FOUR
## WAVELENGTHS

A facsimile, restimulated by the preclear's attention units, can contain enough force to bow his back out of shape, scar his flesh, give him actual electrical shocks or make him hot enough to run a fever, to say nothing of changing his ideas.

Theta can be forced to have a facsimile it did not create. Hit a man, operate on him, beat him, give him a shock–he will then have a facsimile which can reactivate when his attention units, later on, accidentally sweep over it.

However, theta, to be made to have and hold any facsimile, must be "built down." *The only reason theta will hold to a facsimile, the only mechanical way it can hold any facsimile is by having it attached to theta itself.*

We can see that facsimiles are unnecessary, restrictive and, in short, are control mechanisms. To control anyone it is necessary to do one of two things:

1. To give him a basic facsimile strong enough to put him in pain if he fails to obey it.

2. To build on such heavy facsimiles.

For example, a dog is beaten for barking and told to be quiet. Afterwards it is only necessary to tell him to be quiet. This is both operations in one.

In the case of a man–much sturdier stuff than a dog–it requires a *very* heavy facsimile as a basic and facsimiles such as operations, accidents, beatings have to have, as a basic, facsimiles so strong their counterpart cannot as yet be duplicated on Earth. And the basic facsimile must answer a condition–a very important one: *Its wavelengths must have, at least in part, a near approximation of theta itself.*

What wave most closely approximates theta? It would be one of nearly infinite length and that wave is found to be aesthetics, the wavelength of the arts.

Reason, analytical waves, are too coarse to attain theta's 0 or $\infty$ "wavelength." Art alone may do so.

The proof of all this is its workability. And it works. We have then:

Aesthetics

Reason

Emotion

Effort

Matter

To make theta hold a facsimile of emotion or effort or even reason, the facsimile must itself contain an aesthetic wave. The last alone can hold the recordings of pain, grief, exhaustion, aberration, force in upon theta.

If we had to take the emotion, effort and reason or misreason off the whole track, we would have a long task. If we remove the *compulsions* toward aesthetics, we have cut away the only bridge by which heavy facsimiles can be appended to theta. Theta *manufactures* aesthetics. Implanted aesthetic waves, then, if strong enough, could obsess theta into acting on enforced aesthetics.

This *does not* say aesthetics are bad. It says enforced aesthetics are bad. You can't beat a woman into being beautiful. You could beat her into being obsessed about beauty.

Of your free will, that which you see as beautiful gladdens you. Out of an obsessive aberration, all beauty becomes hideous even when the aberree cries out how lovely it is.

# CHAPTER FOUR
## WAVELENGTHS

Just as we have enforced and inhibited ARC, we have enforced and inhibited aesthetics. These, processed, drop off the heavy facsimiles which are thus tied to theta. Process aesthetics and occlusions vanish and current life can be cleared in a few hours.

But what manner of incident is held by an aesthetic wave and how processed? It is so simple.

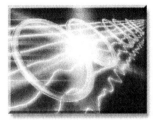

# BLACK AND WHITE

# BLACK AND WHITE

EITHER YOU nor a preclear need accept "whole track" or the identity of the thetan, as described fully in *Scientology: A History of Man.* Not to begin. You'll very rapidly make up your own mind about it, with exclamation points, when you start the process "Black and White."

To audit an "assist," a grief charge, an engram, see earlier works. These items are still with us. That Black and White solves engrams and locks wholesale does not mean single incident running was not effective and that it should not be known. But these and their techniques have no place here in *8-80*.

Single incident processing, Effort Processing and the running of secondaries are all replaced by "Black and White."

Straightwire, Lock Scanning and Valence Shifting are all replaced by "Concept Processing."

The reason for this is that Black and White and Concept Running make Clears, MEST and Theta, in a very short time *and* they are so simple that one cannot mistake any of his moves. And while an auditor can get complete results with them, they do not try his wits. They are 1, 2, 3 processes.

Concept Processing and Black and White mean the goals of Scientology will be reached very soon. And they mean that none in Scientology should be other than a MEST Clear.

As for whole track and thetans, I wouldn't say a word if Black and White didn't show them up with alarming velocity. A preclear can soar so in tone on whole track and Black and White that his capabilities so acquired cannot be ignored even by the bitterest foes of truth and freedom.

As detailed in *Scientology: A History of Man,* there are many electronic implants on the whole track. In other words, any preclear has, in the last few thousand years, been placed in an electronic field and rendered null, void and obsessed by very heavy "electrical" currents.

The object was slavery, a compulsion to be good and obedient and to have a MEST body.

As one makes a dog tame by beating him, one has been made to obey by being beaten with force fields.

A heavy blow gives amnesia. A heavy force field can utterly nullify the entire personalness of a being.

You will not be long in processing before you finally discover, to your own joy, that you are *you*–not a perishable MEST body.

You will find electronic incidents very vicious and so heavy that they push one downscale to a not-beingness which is summed by "I Am Not," "I Know Not." "Disbelief," "Distrust" and many other low-scale concepts rise as you run these heavy incidents.

Somatics of great conviction, however, await your first contact with Black and White.

# CHAPTER FIVE
## BLACK AND WHITE

The electronic fields are ready to be run. They are "in present time." They contain heavy effort and emotion. *And they also contain an aesthetic band. The aesthetic waves alone pin these facsimiles to theta.* You run out the aesthetic wave band and you have run the incident.

# CHAPTER
## SIX

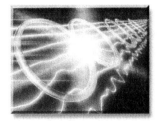

# ℛUNNING BLACK AND WHITE

# RUNNING BLACK AND WHITE

THE RUNNING of Black and White is very simple, simple to do, easy to audit.

The best auditing and the fastest by far is done with the E-Meter. The meter practically runs the case. And, most important, it spares the auditor too close a concentration on his preclear–the only aberrative thing about auditing.

Black and White can be self-audited but in this case the E-Meter becomes quite vital.

Tell any preclear to "see" if he can find a "white area" around him. He will perceive, clearly or weakly, a blackness or a spotty black-whiteness, a grayness or a whiteness around him, above or below him. It may be in patterns or there may be color in it. *You don't want ANYTHING but WHITENESS.*

Tell the preclear to "turn it all white." He will find that if he puts his attention in the center of the sphere, or if he pushes or pulls a little, he can get the field white.

Tell him to "keep it white." He will have to change and shift his attention around in the field, but he can do it. If his attention keeps slipping off, the field will turn black on him. Keep telling him to put his attention back on the place that turns the area around him white.

If you have him on a meter, as you should, you will be able to "read" exactly what is happening.

If the needle steadily climbs to the left (rises), he is keeping the field white. The incident is running out.

If the needle stops or is "sticky," he has a large section of black in the field he must make white. The incident, with black in it, is *not* running out.

If the needle rises and jerks suddenly to the right (drops), he has just gotten a somatic and the suddenness and amount of the drop measure the amount of pain.

To audit, all you do is make him keep the field white. Black spots will appear just before the somatic hits. Theoretically, the entire incident could be run without somatics simply by keeping it white.

The aesthetic wave is all you want out of the incident. This gone, the rest vanishes. It is like having a heavy curtain hanging by a thin strip. Cut the strip and you cut down the whole curtain.

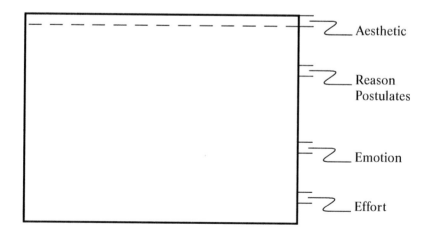

# CHAPTER SIX
## RUNNING BLACK AND WHITE

Run the aesthetic band only. The incident is gone. Run out the heavy electronic incidents and all heavy facsimiles go. For only an electronic can keep a thetan aberrated and form a base "sticky" enough to cause other incidents and locks to stay in present time or restimulate.

When the preclear cannot get the field, an electronic flow is bouncing him. Get his attention to the flow source and keep putting it back every time it bounces until he can manage it. *Or* unburden the case with Concept Running. For if he cannot get white, you must take off some of the "upper" burden of locks by Concept Running.

What of boil-off???

Boil-off, that sinking into grogginess or even unconsciousness, cannot be permitted. It wastes time and does no good. How to stop it?

Your preclear is sending or receiving a white flow. If he stays at it until after he should have reversed it, it goes black and he will start to boil. By quickly shifting the flow of attention or direction of motion in the incident, whiteness returns and the tendency to "boil-off" vanishes.

Hence, by discovering the source of boil-offs and how to stop them we save much time.

@

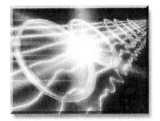

# BLACK AND WHITE AESTHETICS

# CHAPTER SEVEN

# $\mathcal{B}$LACK AND WHITE
# AESTHETICS

*W*HAT DO WE MEAN by aesthetic?

We mean solely and only *Beautiful*.

Beauty is theta. Any wave close to theta is taken by theta for beauty. A harmony of wave motion is evidently a lower harmonic of beauty. A disharmony of wave motion, no matter how high the wavelength, is ugliness. But ugliness is also a wave, a disharmony with the wavelength of beauty* but very close to it.

Light and dark waves, as they appear to attention units, go in harmonics all the way down the scale from .000000000000000000000000002 centimeters to the bottom.

High-wave beauty

High-wave ugliness

It must be remarked that this is an approximation–a rough analogy–for the auditor, not the engineer.

*Honor, gallantry, purity are lower wavelengths. They can be run until beauty is found. –LRH*

*DO NOT GET BEAUTY entangled here with LOVE or anything else but beauty.* Beauty is a wavelength closely resembling theta or a harmony approximating theta. Ugliness is a disharmony in wave discord with theta.

Theta will stop ugliness or disharmony or try to stop it; that is to say, the wave of ugliness will disrupt theta.

This may sound quite poetic. It is in fact very "hard-boiled" engineering. It is just a matter of wavelengths, apparently.

Thus an incident *must* have a beauty factor if it is to append itself to theta. Or it must be underlain by an incident with such a beauty factor.

The "beauty" in this case, and where we will find it to audit, is actually a counterfeit of theta, an obsessive beauty which enforces beauty and forbids ugliness. Theta, left alone, will seek beauty and fight or shun ugliness. It would have to be able to if it could be aberrated into an obsession about beauty. That this obsession is present, an auditing test leaves no doubt.

If your preclear will run the concept of beauty in the white of an electronic incident and the concept of ugliness on the black if it *insists* on coming in, the incident will run out.

Direct the preclear's attention to the white and have him get the concept that it is beautiful. He will not have to employ much effort to keep it white if he keeps this concept.

If the black keeps encroaching, have him run the concept of ugliness on it. It will lose force.

Some preclears are so badly aberrated that black has become the only desirable shade. Here is the criminal. The preclear can run how beautiful black is. He won't do it for long.

The original incidents, when they were laid in, were designed to be obsessive. Most have the beauty-ugly motive. This makes the victim obsessed to keep all calm and not fight. There are even scenes–"*hot* facsimiles," pictures made of raw energy–to show him beauty. As if theta had no concept.

The other twin which a preclear gets in some incidents is good-evil. Good is a rational level wave, a harmonic on beauty, much lower. It evolves up into beauty when run and should to get the incident free. Evil, of course, is as black as white is good. Religious obsessive incidents (complete with religious scenes) come in easily and run, when the white is run, with the concept "good." This soon goes upscale to beauty.

All electronic incidents run out on Black and White with the concept of "beauty" and with a placing of attention so that the white turns on as bright as possible.

These incidents were intended to be confusing, the better to make a slave obey (they thought). By running half the waves one way and half the other, a beauty-ugly conflict was created.

Back and forth white 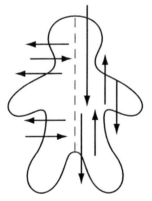 Up and down white

One side appears to go black when the other is run. Just get the concept of beauty and follow the waves and the concept runs out the confusion.

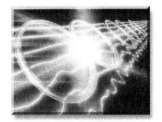

# CONCEPT
# RUNNING

# CONCEPT RUNNING

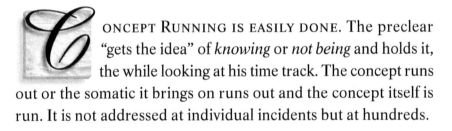

ONCEPT RUNNING IS EASILY DONE. The preclear "gets the idea" of *knowing* or *not being* and holds it, the while looking at his time track. The concept runs out or the somatic it brings on runs out and the concept itself is run. It is not addressed at individual incidents but at hundreds.

A concept is a high-wave *thought,* above perception or reason or single incidents. Thus as concepts are run, many incidents made tumble into view.

Concepts can be "in-run" or "out-run." This would be somebody having the concept of the preclear or the preclear having the concept himself. If the preclear runs a concept and starts to boil-off, have him reverse the flow. If he was running it as his own, have him run it as another's and he will immediately cease the boil-off.

You can have a concept of anything, even a concept of confusion. The top and bottom scales of the Chart of Attitudes make good concept material.

*But* the only concepts we have to use in running out locks or whole lives, knocking away scores of incidents at a time, are:

* Beauty

* Ugliness

* Cause of Ugliness

* Cause of Beauty

* No-Sympathy

* Sympathy

* Good

* Evil

Wherever there is an occlusion on a case, make the preclear run these on it. Wherever the scenery or people are too bright or fixed, have him run these on it.

That's all.

*(Start, stop, change, attainment, inability to reach)* –LRH

# CHAPTER NINE

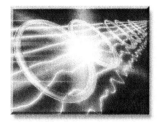

# ODIES

 OU CAN RUN Beauty and Ugliness on parts of the body, on people in the preclear's past and on the current and former bodies of the preclear.

When you do the last, you will find this pattern showing up in his current body:

*Each line on the
vertical is a ridge left
by some past body.
The ridges, turned white,
bring a visio
of a former body.*

The preclear, as a thetan, diminished in size as time went on. The first impression seems like a very small person, about down to the thighs from the level of the mouth.

The preclear had bodies further away than this.

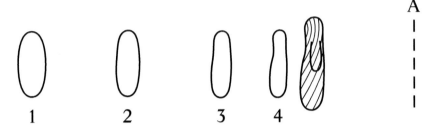

*Decreasing control distance*

If number 2, as an engram, is in restimulation, the preclear will think he is at position A behind himself, whereas he is solidly frozen by aberration into his own MEST body.

To separate the preclear from bodies and discover *why* he thinks he is only the current body, run this about bodies, particularly on old facsimiles of bodies a few feet in front of him:

Non-Sympathy for body

Sympathy for body

Propitiation for body

Being a body

Here he will rapidly recover the sensation of his becoming nothing and the body everything.

Run Beauty-Ugliness on all bodies he had.

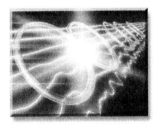

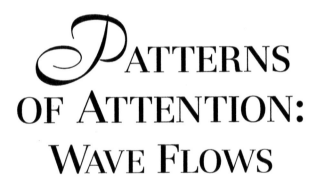

# PATTERNS
# OF ATTENTION:
# WAVE FLOWS

# PATTERNS OF ATTENTION: WAVE FLOWS

 HE PATTERNS OF ATTENTION or wave flows are:

Source

**Simple flow**
Fix attention on Source.

**Explosion/Dispersal**
Sphere or disc out from center.
Fix attention on center then on
the surface, collapsing it.

**Implosion**
Imploding into center.
Fix attention on center then on
surface, getting out from it.

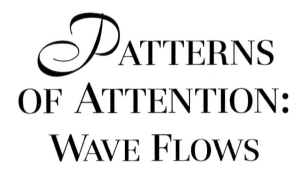

**A retractor wave**
Put attention on both directions
at once.

Work on all flows until they turn white.

For everything that you find happened to the preclear, he did
something like it to another.

Run any incident until it seems "sticky." Then run the opposite. Back and forth as required. Incidents run, then, first the motivator or DEDEX, then the overt or DED.

For every inflow there is an outflow in all present time locked facsimiles. Any flow run until it goes black will turn white or erase when the direction of flow is reversed.

When any part of the body puts out in a single direction only or too long, it will aberrate.

The thetan puts in the wave of beauty into bodies, gets back low level or sex (just below beauty). The thetan doesn't get a beauty wave back from bodies. Putting out too long, the thetan keys in the "beauty" counterfeit of a facsimile. Thus electronic incidents come into play. Run the thetan putting out or failing to put out beauty into bodies and situations.

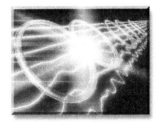

AN AUDITING
FORMULA

# $\mathscr{A}$N AUDITING FORMULA

$\mathscr{A}$N AUDITING FORMULA to make a Theta Clear.

1. Read questions to preclear from *Handbook for Preclears* until auditor has confidence.

2. Run Beauty-Ugly current life until all occlusions gone.

3. Run by Black and White any electronic incident which shows up while doing (2). Alternate such incidents with current life until current life clears.

4. Run all Blanketings.

5. Run most distant body preclear can contact. Run out.

6. Run closer and closer bodies until preclear is Clear.

# PART

"The most important step in establishing
a preclear's self-determinism,
the main goal of the auditor,

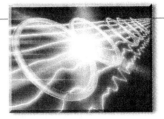

# T w o

*August 1952*

*is the rehabilitation of the preclear's*
*ability to produce energy."*

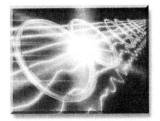

# THE
# DICHOTOMIES

# THE DICHOTOMIES

HILE THE AUDITOR can do much solely by reducing facsimiles, he soon will find that his preclears are not always able to erase facsimiles easily. He will find, occasionally, that he often has a difficult time when a particularly heavy facsimile is in restimulation. And do what he will, the auditor may find his preclear's tone remains unchanged and that the preclear's attitudes have not evolved to a better high.

We now come to "The Governor," mentioned in a lecture in the autumn of 1951. The speed of a preclear is the speed of his production of energy.

The most important step in establishing a preclear's self-determinism, the main goal of the auditor, is the rehabilitation of the preclear's ability to produce energy.

A being is apparently an energy production source. How does he produce live energy without mechanical means, cellular activity, or food?

The basic principle of energy production by a being has been copied in electronics. It is very simple. A difference of potential of two areas can establish an energy flow of themselves. Carbon batteries, electric generators and other producers of electrical flows act on the principle that a difference of energy potential in two or more areas can cause an electrical impulse to flow between or amongst them.

The preclear is static and kinetic, meaning he is no-motion and motion. These, interplaying, produce electrical flow.

A preclear, as a static, can hold two or more energy flows of different wavelengths in proximity and between them obtain a flow.

A preclear can hold a difference of flow between two waves and a static so long (and arduously) that the effect of a discharging condenser can be obtained. This can "explode" a facsimile.

The preclear flows electrical currents of command at the body. These hit pre-established ridges (areas of dense waves) and cause the body to perceive or act. The preclear takes perception from the body with tractor beams. He holds the body still or braces himself against it by wrapping a "tractor" (pulling) beam around it while he places a "pressor" (pushing) beam at his back to command himself into action. (You can almost break a preclear's spine by asking him to contact his own tractor around his body and yet withhold the pressor against his spine.)

# Chapter Twelve
## The Dichotomies

All an auditor really needs to know about this is the elementary method of using a difference of potential. That creates energy.

The only thing wrong with a preclear with an aged MEST body is that he has too many facsimiles of his tractors and pressors handling his own MEST body. And the rickety state of the body feeds back "slowness" so that he thinks his energy is low and, until worked with some method such as this, facsimiles do not reduce.

*Any* difference of potential, played one against the other, creates energy. Aesthetic waves against a static produce energy. Aesthetic waves against analytical waves produce energy. Analytical waves against emotional waves produce energy. Emotional waves against effort waves produce energy. Effort against matter produces energy.

The last is the method used on Earth in generating electrical current for power. The others are equally valid and produce even higher flows. This is a gradient scale of beingness, from the zero-infinity of theta to the solidity of matter.

The differences of potential most useful are easy to run.

This is, actually, alternating current (AC) running. There can be DC running or chain fission running, but these are very experimental at this writing.

AC is created by the static holding first one, then the other, of a dichotomy of two differences of potential. A flow is run in one direction with one of the pair, then in the other direction with the other.

The dichotomies are:

1. Survive
   Succumb
2. Affinity
   No affinity
3. Communication
   No communication
4. Agree
   Disagree
5. Start
   Stop
6. Be
   Not be
7. Know
   Know not
8. Cause
   Effect
9. Change
   No change
10. Win
    Lose
11. I am
    I am not
12. Faith
    Distrust
13. Imagine
    Truth
14. Believe
    Not believe
15. Always
    Never
16. Future
    Past

17. Everybody
    Nobody
18. Owns all
    Owns nothing
19. Responsible
    Not responsible
20. Right
    Wrong
21. Stay
    Escape
22. Beauty
    Ugliness
23. Reason
    Emotion
24. Emotion
    Effort
25. Effort
    Apathy
26. Acceptance
    Rejection
27. Sane
    Insane
28. No-sympathy
    Sympathy
29. Sympathy
    Propitiation

And the state of Static, a motionlessness sometimes necessary to run.

## CHAPTER TWELVE
## THE DICHOTOMIES

How are these used?

One asks the preclear to flow agreement, then disagreement. He flows a feeling, a thought (never the phrase!) of "agreement," out or in, in the direction he chooses relative to himself. He lets this flow until it turns smoky gray or white, then black. Then he changes the direction of flow and gets the thought or feeling of "disagreement." He runs this until it turns gray or white, then black. When this has turned black or dark, he again runs "agreement" in its direction until he gets gray or white, then again black. Now he reverses the flow and flows the thought "disagreement" until he gets gray or white, then blackness. And so on and on.

It will be noted that at first it may take some little time for a flow to run from black through white to black. As the preclear continues to run, after minutes or many hours, he begins to run faster, then faster and faster, until at last he can keep a flow blazing and crackling.

A method of aberrating beings was to give them white and black energy sources in their vicinity. These show up on a very low-tone occluded case as blazing white and shining white. That is an electronic incident, not his own energy flow. These run blazing white *in one direction* for minutes or hours before they go black. They then run the other way, blazing white, almost as long.

*When black predominates in such incidents, they do not diminish or reduce. Ask the preclear, in such a case, to do what he "has to do" to get the incident all white.*

As the preclear runs, he finds the speed of the change of flow changes more and more rapidly until it runs like a vibration.

This vibration, theoretically, can increase to a strong current which becomes so great it is well to *ground* your preclear by using an E-Meter or letting him hold a wire in each hand which is connected to a bare water pipe or radiator. Otherwise, his MEST body may be damaged by the flow.

Run a dichotomy only against its mate. Run in alternating directions until the flow turns black.

Don't run a black "flow." It doesn't flow or run out.

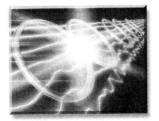

# SELF-DETERMINISM
# OTHER-DETERMINISM

# $\mathscr{S}$ELF-DETERMINISM
# $\mathscr{O}$THER-DETERMINISM

 ELF-DETERMINISM is whiteness and self-made energy to the preclear. The energy looks white to him.

Self-determinism
Other-determinism

is the basic dichotomy. The self-determinism looks white, other-determinism looks black.

Electronic incidents are a mockery of this. They made the preclear think his own determinism had *other* determinism it must fight. White beauty must fight black ugliness. White good must fight black evil.

You will sometimes see your preclear is *fighting, pushing, struggling* instead of getting flows. He has encountered a black mock-up which he thinks he has to fight. This is the aberration–that one is not Eighth Dynamic Cause but is only First Dynamic Cause.

To become free he must be Cause, as nearly as possible, on eight dynamics. He cannot be fully responsible–and thus, not responsible–for his facsimiles unless he is *Cause.* If he is not responsible for his facsimiles, he then can be injured by them, can be the Effect of *their* Cause.

One requires the preclear, in such a case of *fighting,* to run the dichotomy, not just strain at the black. He may protest, saying he "cannot accept it." Ask him to run "acceptance" anyway, or get him into something lighter.

At first your preclear may be unable even to find gray. In such a case, get him to pretend somebody is before him saying something to him. Ask him to run the flow of his own agreement. Then ask him to run his own flow of disagreement. Shortly he will sense how long he must run each. Even if he runs only on this conceptual level, he will improve markedly in tone and, of course, energy potential.

Your preclear must be able to recognize a *tractor,* a pulling wave, and realize that it has two directions of flow. As you point out that he has a tractor-pressor combination on his MEST body, he probably can find it. You can point out that other persons have put them on his body and that he has put them on others. He will find how to make them flow–for the tractor is just a holder so that a pressor can be used, or a puller to make someone fall or stop somebody or something from falling.

The only one he would not find for himself is the tractor he gives others to make them want things from him and tractors they have extended to him to make him want things from them. These last lead straight into art and the Second Dynamic.

# SELF-DETERMINISM — OTHER-DETERMINISM

The most important dichotomies to run are:

Agree
Disagree

Beauty
Ugliness

But all those listed are useful. However, do not force him to use and try to prevent him from using:

Emotion
Effort

Effort
Matter

These fall away of themselves, evidently, when the others are run.

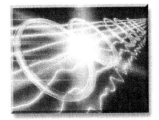

# EMOTIONAL CONCEPTS AND BRACKETS

# EMOTIONAL CONCEPTS AND BRACKETS

 HERE ARE CERTAIN emotional concepts which are very effective and should be used.

One *holds* one of these concepts and agrees and disagrees with it. He holds the concept and gets the flow on it by agreeing and disagreeing on the concept of subjects to keep them gray or white.

The concept of beauty is run by holding the idea of a "beautiful state of affairs" and then agreeing and disagreeing (to keep gray or white) on the locks and flows which turn up.

Similarly, one handles the following concepts:

Ugliness

Beautiful sadness

Degradation

No-sympathy

Sympathy

Propitiation

Making amends

Guilt

Hiding

Exhibitionism

Beautiful cruelty

The beautiful sadness of losing

The beautiful sadness of any dichotomy

The beauty of winning

The beauty of any dichotomy

The desire of any dichotomy

The inhibition of any dichotomy

One runs things as close to thought as possible and as far from effort.

One runs things in *brackets*.

# EMOTIONAL CONCEPTS AND BRACKETS

The word "bracket" is taken from the artillery, meaning "to enclose within a salvo of fire."

A bracket is run as follows:

First, one gets the concept as *happening to the preclear.*

Then, one gets the concept of *the preclear making it happen (or thinking or saying it) to another.*

Then, one gets the concept as *being directed by another at others.*

Then, one uses all these on the other side of the dichotomy.

A bracket on "Beauty of being an individual" would be as follows:

*"Get how beautiful it is for you to be an individual."*

When he has run this for a while, keeping it gray or white by agreeing or disagreeing with the flows:

*"Get how beautiful it is for others to be an individual."*

He runs this until he isn't very interested, changing its flows by agreeing or disagreeing, and then:

*"Get how beautiful people think it is for others to be individuals."*

Again, he holds the concept and runs the agreement and disagreement to get flows. Now:

*"Get how ugly it is to be an individual."*

He holds this concept and gets the flows as they come, agreement and disagreement:

*"Get how ugly it is for another to be an individual."*

*"Get how ugly people think it is for people to be individuals."*

This is a full bracket. It can be done with any dichotomy. The standard bracket, the one you will use most, is based on beauty and ugliness with agree and disagree as the flow concepts and with the other dichotomies as the varied thought.

If your preclear can get no concept on beauty, have him run the Tone Scale on it as follows, having him agree and disagree to get a flow:

Apathy about beauty (motionless)

Grief about beauty

Fear of beauty

Resentment of beauty

Anger at beauty

Antagonism toward beauty

Boredom about beauty

Conservatism about beauty

Enthusiasm about beauty

Exhilaration about beauty

Run this scale wherever he can get it and then continue to run it on the others until he has at last become able to get the feeling of beauty. He will get "being taught" what is beautiful or trying to "understand" beauty and many other concepts.

Your preclear may run into a heavy electronic incident. These are covered fully in *Scientology: A History of Man*. If he does, you can run it by getting him to "turn it white" and "keep it white." If he can't, get him into lighter material.

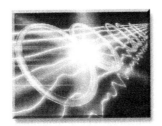

# PRECLEARS AND BODIES

# PRECLEARS AND BODIES

THE REASON your preclear is fixed to a MEST body lies in his inability to produce energy enough to know and to get away from one.

His career with bodies is as follows:

*He hurt them by accident first.*

*Then he hurt them without understanding they hurt by using their sexual emotion.*

*Then he blamed them and said and felt he would have no responsibility for them.*

*Then he felt the emotion of no-sympathy for them.*

*Then he felt sympathy.*

*He began to propitiate.*

*He wanted to make amends.*

*He* was *a MEST body.*\*

Run the beauty and ugliness of these.

The cycle of no-sympathy-equals-sympathy is inevitable. That for which we declare no-sympathy today will receive our sympathy tomorrow.

If you have a preclear sight some old body well before him and feel no-sympathy for it, he then will feel no-sympathy, sympathy, propitiation and, suddenly, he *is* the body.

One runs facsimiles on the body partly because the body is an electrical ground, partly because it has been assigned responsibility.

The thetan assigning responsibility to the body then *becomes* the body. This is a general principle. One *becomes* that to which he assigns responsibility too often and too long. He makes it *Cause* and, at last, to be *Cause* himself, he must be the thing.

\**The cycle no-sympathy, sympathy, propitiation, make-amends, beingness IS the cause and cycle of the life continuum. It accounts in part for the transfer of somatics in an overt act or DED. It is a therapy in itself. It is run by itself but better with the concepts of beauty and ugliness, with agree and disagree on each level of the cycle. You could give this to a practitioner by itself and he would become quite famous for relieving aches and pains, for it solves valences, the acquirement of family difficulties from parents and a thousand other things. The cycle sometimes runs anger, no-sympathy, fear, sympathy, propitiation, make-amends, beingness. The anger factor is the holder in the incident (and has tractors with it) and the fear is a bouncer. Fear of punishment is largely the fear in this cycle during the actual act, not afterwards because of police. No-sympathy is an emotion and an action. One puts a black curtain before himself to prevent his feeling affinity with that which he is hurting. This is a motionlessness which turns gray and runs out on agree and disagree from the victim and the punisher. No-sympathy can be an occlusion for the whole track. No-sympathy is also, of course, counter-no-sympathy in many incidents. –LRH*

# CHAPTER FIFTEEN
## PRECLEARS AND BODIES

People imagine they are in bodies because they are hiding from something and many other reasons. But these are not important. The important thing is that bodies were handy to have, once. They were fun.

This process, as itself, as simple as it is, will eventually detach one from his body. After that, he can use it or not as he chooses.

The thetan is no fairy tale. Try these techniques for fifty hours and find out. Try them on a preclear who has never heard of facsimiles, electronics or whole track and in fifty or one hundred hours he will be outside wondering what he was doing in "that thing"! You may have intended only to increase his sanity or happiness. You do it best by processing the *thetan* on 8-80.

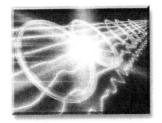

# THE
# SUB-ZERO
# TONE SCALE

# THE SUB-ZERO TONE SCALE

ELOW ZERO ON THE TONE SCALE is applicable only to a thetan.

It has been quite commonly observed that there are two positions for any individual on the Tone Scale. This occurs because there is a position for the composite of the thetan plus his MEST body, operating in a state of unknowingness that he is not a MEST body and behaving according to social patterns which give him some semblance of sanity. The other position on the Tone Scale is the position of the thetan himself and it is necessary for us to demonstrate a negative scale in order to find the thetan at all.

For the thetan, you will find the scale as follows:

| Thetan Scale Range | | |
|---|---|---|
| Well below body death at "0.0" down to complete unbeingness as a thetan | 40.0 | Serenity of beingness |
| | 20.0 | Action |
| | 8.0 | Exhilaration |
| | 4.0 | Enthusiasm |
| **Thetan-Plus-Body** Social training and education sole guarantee of sane conduct | 3.0 | Conservatism |
| | 2.5 | Boredom |
| | 2.0 | Antagonism |
| | 1.8 | Pain |
| | 1.5 | Anger |
| | 1.2 | No-sympathy |
| | 1.0 | Fear |
| | 0.9 | Sympathy |
| | 0.8 | Propitiation |
| | 0.5 | Grief |
| | 0.375 | Making amends |
| | 0.05 | Apathy |
| | 0.0 | Being a body |
| | -0.2 | Being other bodies |
| | -1.0 | Punishing other bodies |
| | -1.3 | Responsibility as blame |
| | -1.5 | Controlling bodies |
| | -2.2 | Protecting bodies |
| | -3.0 | Owning bodies |
| | -3.5 | Approval from bodies |
| | -4.0 | Needing bodies |
| | -8.0 | Hiding |

# CHAPTER SIXTEEN
## THE SUB-ZERO TONE SCALE

This Sub-zero Tone Scale shows that the thetan is several bands below knowingness as a body–and so he will be found in the majority of cases. In our Homo sapiens, he will be discovered to be below zero on the Tone Scale. The 0.0 to 4.0-plus Tone Scale was formulated on and referred to bodies and the activity of thetans with bodies. In order, then, to discover the state of mind of the thetan, one must examine the Sub-zero Scale. He has some trained patterns as a body which make it possible for him to *know* and to *be*. As himself, he has lost all beingness, all pride, all memories and all self-determined ability, but yet has an automatic-response mechanism in himself which continues furnishing his energy.

*Each one of the above points on the scale is run as positive and negative!*

Example: The beautiful sadness of needing bodies, the beautiful sadness of *not* needing bodies. The beauty of being responsible for bodies, the beauty of *not* being responsible for bodies. Each one is run as itself and then as the reverse with the addition of *not*.

The Sub-zero to 40.0 Scale is the range of the thetan. A thetan is lower than body death, since it survives body death. It is in a state of knowingness below 0.375 only when it is identifying itself as a body and *is*, to its own thinking, the body. The Body-Plus-Thetan Scale is from 0.0 to 4.0 and the position on this scale is established by the social environment and education of the composite being and is a stimulus-response scale. The preclear is initially above this 0.375 on the Body-Plus-Thetan range. Then, on auditing, he commonly drops from the false tone of the Body-Plus-Thetan Scale and into the true tone of the thetan.

This is actually the only self-determined tone present–the actual tone of the thetan. From this Sub-zero, he quickly rises upscale through the entire range, as a thetan, and generally settles at 20.0 and in command of the body and situations. The course of auditing, then, takes the preclear, quite automatically, down from the *false tone* of the Body-Plus-Thetan Scale to the *actual tone* of the thetan. Then the tone of the thetan rises back up the scale level by level.

It is not uncommon to find the preclear (who *is* the thetan) quite raving mad under the false "veneer" of social and educational stimulus-response training. And to discover that the preclear, while behaving quite normally in the Body-Plus-Thetan state, becomes irrational in the course of auditing. *But despite this,* the preclear is actually being far more sane and rational than ever before. And the moment he discovers himself as himself, as *the* source of energy and personality and beingness of a body, he becomes physically and mentally better. Thus the auditor must not be dismayed at the course of tone, but should simply persevere until he has the thetan up into rational range. A raving mad thetan is far more sane than a normal human being. But then, as you audit, observe it for yourself.

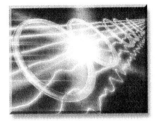

# THE MANIFESTATIONS
# OF ENERGY

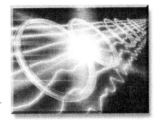

# THE MANIFESTATIONS OF ENERGY

# THE MANIFESTATIONS OF ENERGY

THE MANIFESTATIONS OF ENERGY are three in number. These are: "flow," "dispersal" and "ridges."

Utilizing flows, dispersals and ridges, there are several patterns of life energy. These include "pressor beams," "tractor beams" and "screens." The screen is actually a ridge that is formed for a special purpose of protection.

Any line of flow, whether contracting or lengthening, is called a flow. A common manifestation is seen in an electric light wire.

A dispersal is formed by a source emanating. This may or may not be an explosion. Any source with a multiple direction emanation can be called a dispersal.

A ridge is caused by two energy flows coinciding and causing an enturbulence of energy which on examination is found to take on a characteristic which, in energy flows, is very like matter, having its particles in chaotic mixture.

A particular type of dispersal is a "reverse dispersal," or an "implosion."

As an illustration, a beam of light would be emanating from a source-point and flowing toward something to be seen. Striking a reverse flow, it can form a ridge. Striking a solid object, it would form on the face of that object a ridge.

All energy behaviors are manifestations of these characteristics of energy.

Energy is subdivisible into a large motion–such as a flow, a dispersal or a ridge–and a small motion, which is itself commonly called a "particle" in nuclear physics.

Agitation within agitation is the basic formation of particles of energy, such as electrons, protons and others. These are not, as their Greek name "atom" once told us about the atom, indivisible. Energy flows have many forms and each form is reducible to a smaller vibration.

The characteristics of any vibration are that it contains the manifestations of a static and a kinetic. A static is something with no motion, no particle and no wavelength. And a kinetic is something which has considerable motion. The interplay between the static and one or more kinetics causes energy interchanges.

The entire principle of alternating currents, as drawn in most books on electricity, is in error. This shows a positive terminal and a negative terminal, discharging one against the other, rotationally, so as to create an alternating current flow. As part of Scientology, it is originated that the principle is in error by the fact that the negative terminal must have a plus negative and the positive terminal must have a negative positive to form such an interchange. Past technology, in describing the alternating current flow and the describing of all energy manifestations and manufactures, forgets continually the base. This is represented in an electrical generator by the base of the generator itself. The solid iron base of the generator, fastened to a floor or table, imposes time and space upon the two terminals. Without this imposition of time and space, no energy could be possible. A great deal of mechanical motion must be put into an electrical generator because an electrical generator is discharging between the dichotomy of *effort* and *matter,* a lower-ranged dichotomy. In the higher ranges, the static is furnished by the individual and the mathematical symbol for this near-ultimate is *theta* ($\theta$).

Self-determinism is entirely and solely the imposition of time and space upon energy flows. Imposing time and space upon objects, people, self, events and individuals is Causation. The total components of his self-determinism are the ability to impose time and space. His energy is derived from the discharge of high and low, or different, potentials to which he has assigned time and space. Dwindling sanity is a dwindling ability to assign time and space. Psychosis is a complete inability to assign time and space. This is, as well, willpower.

In life, one finds the static operating against the kinetic of the material universe which itself has motion. A static takes pictures of the motion which it can place and reactivate at will. It uses these pictures of motion as terminals. The types of motion in the terminals discharge one against the other in accordance with the experience desired by the life force.

Relative speeds determine potential.

The speed of light is not a constant of energy speed. The shorter the period of emission of energy from a source–which is to say, the shorter the wavelength of the energy–the greater is the speed of that energy. As one ranges up the Tone Scale, one comes into the near instantaneousness of thought. And very high on the Tone Scale, one finds thought so close to the static that the static is capable of assigning the thought *with* the time–into the past and into the future–without regard to the time factor imposed upon the MEST universe, also evidently by some such static.

Far from some mystic concept, the static and kinetic principles of energy interchange can be fundamental to nuclear physics. "Attention units" are actually energy flows of small wavelengths and definite frequency. These are measurable on specially designed oscilloscopes and meters. No special particle is involved, but one can designate the particle of such flows as "corbitrons," if one desires to be technical.

The constant of light has been a sort of scientific ridge locking scientific thought. Within the spectrum of light itself, there is a measurable difference of speed. And in the higher spectrum of reason and aesthetics, the speed of light is very fast. On the other hand, the speed of emotion, which is a gross wave, is evidently quite slow.

One can conceive of an ultimate static, which would be theta, and an ultimate motion, which would be MEST. The interplay to create energy, however, can be much narrower. One has observed preclears try to run pleasure and find only pain. One has observed them run pain and find pleasure, but less often. The direct current and condenser discharges are determined by wave characteristic. One can create a pleasure facsimile and discharge pain into it, a primary function of imagination.

The life source itself *IS* energy. The energy potential of beings can be varied slightly within one being and is quite different from individual to individual as a basic quality.

The life source of the individual is interior in most persons because it has built up, with its earlier flows, ridges which themselves have the same wavelength as the life source of the person. The life source, then, cannot distinguish between himself and these ridges. These ridges are facsimiles, or pictures, of motion. They are used by the life source to turn the body into a stimulus-response, or automatic, mechanism. By means of such ridges, the life source can turn the body into an automaton which will operate for him. However, as the life source goes down Tone Scale, it itself can become enturbulated and less able to impose time and space upon his facsimiles. He cannot distinguish between himself and a ridge which is an apparent identity.

The name given to this life source is "thetan." It is the individual, the being, the personality, the knowingness of the human being.

The state of the human being is artificial, the thetan using the body for his own pleasure and convenience. A thetan, having done so, ordinarily forgets he is doing so. And, in order to increase his randomity, initially suppresses the fact that he is separate from the body. He then becomes identified with the body to such a degree that should the body die, he abandons to it (he supposes, but not actually) all the facsimiles which have been accumulated for that body.

If the preclear refers to "his thetan," he has not identified himself, since he supposes his thetan to be something else or elsewhere. He *is* the thetan and, when he is in a state of knowingness, he knows *where* he is. If he is in a state of unknowingness (which is to say, identified with the body), he does not know where he is.

When a thetan has come down Tone Scale to the minus scale, he no longer believes himself capable of the production of power, he cannot select facsimiles for interchanges and he becomes an unknowingly motivating portion of the person. But all the person ever will be *is* the thetan.

The genetic entity is of very little concern.

These manifestations of energy, and the life source, can be discovered easily by the technique which has now been developed.

The formula of the energy of life source which has been tentatively advanced is:

$$\text{Life} = \frac{EI}{-R} \cdot (-f)$$

*If:*

E = Energy Potential
I = Energy Flow
-R = Negative Resistance
-f = Negative Frequency

The theory of the "counter-elasticity of flow" is easily observed on an oscilloscope and is possibly the negative frequency. An energy line will flow, whether in space or in a confined conduit, just so long before it accumulates sufficient enturbulence to stop. It requires, then, an enormous forcing potential behind it to continue its flow. This is resistance (and is, indeed, the resistance in electrical wires) and is one of the main reasons why power has to be furnished to a generator. The flow, when it has gone to the limit of the elasticity of the particles it contains, will then discharge backwards against its direction of flow (and, if agitated, will do so). A flow must flow in one direction and then in the reverse direction, and within the limits of the elasticity of flow, in order to create an energy which does not require heavy potentials to keep it in flow.

While the "conservation of energy" is a useful principle in basic physics and elementary nuclear physics (such as those used in the creation of the atom bomb and in the formulas of Lorentz-FitzGerald), its practical application is demonstrable only between effort and matter on the Tone Scale and is useful within the bounds of mechanical motion and activity in the material universe only. That thought may be seen occasionally to violate the conservation of energy does not immediately cancel the fact that thought is part of the material universe and is as much energy as electrons, protons and electric lights. Thought is self-perpetuating, so long as it operates in the bands above emotion. When it falls below the band of emotion, it ceases to perpetuate itself.

There is much technology here which has been discovered with relationship to energy and the material universe. And these principles are applicable to such things as the creation of weapons which will cancel or explode, at a distance, the force of an atom bomb. Or which will themselves, at a cost of two or three hundred dollars, make automatic firing blasts on the level of an atomic explosion. Nuclear physics has been in its infancy and a great deal of pioneer work has been possible in the field. It should not be considered that nuclear physics has invaded the field of life any more than the humanities have invaded the field of life. Energy manifestations have a single applicable pattern. And those patterns apply as well to thought as they apply to electrical flows. It is simply that we have advanced a technology toward a logical conclusion and have obtained logical results.

These results are revealed, at this time, only because they can be demonstrated easily with oscilloscopes, with groundings, with the manufacture of energy and in the field of humanities, most importantly, with the restoration of life energy and vitality to human beings–with according enhancement of sanity and activity.

# PART

"The technique is simple, but it is
who has a thorough command

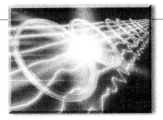

# *T* H R E E

*September 1952*

*most simple to an individual
of the entire subject."*

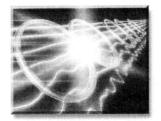

# PHENOMENA OF THE THETAN

# PHENOMENA OF THE THETAN

HETAN IS THE WORD given to the awareness of awareness unit, the life source, the personality and the beingness of Homo sapiens. It is derived from the symbol *theta,* θ, a Greek letter. It is *not* somebody else, a thing one has, a soul, a spirit. It *is* the person. One does not speak of "my" thetan. This would be a circuit. One would speak of "me." *Me* means to aberrated persons the *Body-Plus-Thetan. Me* should mean *THETAN ONLY.*

The thetan is a glowing unit of energy source. He seems, to himself, to be anything from a quarter of an inch to two inches in diameter. His capability is *knowing* and *being.* He exudes and uses energy in many forms. He can perceive and handle energy flows easily.

The thetan enters sometime in early infancy. This may be before, during or following birth.

He comes in a state of personal unknowingness, desiring to have an identity which he considers that he has not without a body.

He throws capping beams at the genetic entity, takes over the body.

He now does a life continuum for the body. His taking it over is an overt act he afterwards hides even from himself.

This incident must be run.

The thetan, in most preclears, is within the skull. It shifts on auditing (which is to say, the preclear shifts) from behind to in front of the head. But it is always itself. On many preclears, the thetan has so many ridges around him that he disperses all through them. This dispersion is done along communication lines. When the dispersion is audited out, the thetan is a unit as above.

Standing behind the body, the thetan can adjust and change any error in the body at will. He sees these as black spots. To get rid of them, one has only to get the flows necessary to make and keep them white. Some thetans immediately gain the ability to discharge energy at will. When a thetan discharges energy, another person may feel hot.

The thetan collapses into the body when the body feels pain. This was how he got trapped. Auditing must resolve this.

A thetan can get partly outside himself on a ridge. Then the preclear seems to be inside himself and yet outside. The answer in this case is to work the thetan from inside the head, getting him to blow out ridges with beams. Just on straight beauty and ugliness on the Sub-zero Scale, getting concepts and feelings, the thetan eventually will come outside. But this *may* take a very long time, even as much as two or three hundred hours. The techniques of the next chapter are faster. Bring the thetan outside and work him. Then he has his own identity.

## CHAPTER EIGHTEEN
## PHENOMENA OF THE THETAN

The thetan *is* the preclear. The Body-Plus-Thetan is no increase of personality. The body is a sort of vegetable run by the genetic entity.

The thetan can clean up and heal his own body and those of others at will.

The thetan is usually either blind or very dim-sighted at first. He gradually regains his ability to perceive as he comes up the Tone Scale. He passes a band of dub-in above 0.0 and below 2.0. He attains clear, brilliant sight higher on the scale.

One does not audit engrams with the thetan. He blows ridges to which are fastened thousands of engrams. This is very fast auditing. Ridges are blown by locating them and turning them white. If they don't blow at first glance, get the flow in and the flow out from the thetan, alternating it, until the ridge is continually gray or white and, by shifting flows, keep it so until it is gone. After flowing gray or white in one direction for a short time, a ridge goes black. Then the flow is reversed and the ridge goes white or gray again. If it then turns black, once more reverse the flow. The ridges can act like beings when sprayed with energy or when permitted to give off energy. These are the "demon circuits of the mind."

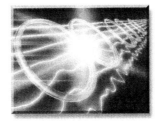

# SUMMARY OF TECHNIQUE 8-80: RUNNING THE THETAN

# CHAPTER NINETEEN

# SUMMARY OF TECHNIQUE 8-80: RUNNING THE THETAN

THE SUMMARY TECHNIQUE of the running of the thetan is very simple and quick. The thetan is in apathy. Therefore, like a child who will no longer ask for that which will not be given him, he negates as his fastest response.

The entire technique consists of getting the thetan out of the body immediately, unburdening some of the sympathy for the body and, by running brackets, using the Sub-zero Tone Scale, bringing him up to complete self-determinism, at which time he can handle the body with great ease.

As far as psychosomatic illnesses are concerned–derangements of the body, malformations, malfunctions–the thetan can care for these with great ease once he has been brought up the Tone Scale. He will care for them automatically and put the body into excellent condition.

That most thetans, the moment they find themselves out of the body, desire to have nothing further to do with it is an aberrated condition, just as it is an aberrated condition for a thetan to be fixed on having nothing to do with anything *but* bodies.

One runs each point of the Sub-zero Scale as a dichotomy–which is to say, Punishment-No-punishment, Owning-Not-owning, Controlling-Not-controlling, Being-Not-being. He runs these as concepts. He runs them most opportunely with the thetan outside the body, for the thetan then is not enturbulated by all the facsimiles and ridges which he finds in his vicinity.

*The technique is as follows:*

The preclear is asked to be or not be a short distance behind his head. From this position, he is then asked to feel a very little bit of sympathy for the body. (Feeling too much may make the preclear feel as though his head were being torn off.) The person is then asked to scan out the small action of moving out of the body and into the body–and scan it out while out of the body. The next steps are repetitions of these. But it will be found that the dichotomies and the beautiful sadness of each dichotomy must be run to bring the thetan up into a state of knowingness.

The thetan, about half the time, will respond to a negative command, where he will not respond to a positive command.

Occasionally, a person must be audited by running facsimiles before he can be placed in a situation where he can leave the body, but in most cases this will not be necessary. It, however, is necessary on occasion for the auditor to run facsimiles. And, in any event, he should know all he can discover about facsimiles, manifestations of the body, entities and other matters contained in the body of Scientology, or otherwise he will find phenomena which he will possibly misconstrue.

The facsimiles in the body are fastened onto ridges. These ridges generally appear black to the thetan. They will turn white if the individual is asked to find out what the ridge is saying. And then the individual is asked to own it, or remove it, and the ridge or black spot will turn white and disappear–often with a considerable somatic. These ridges are discovered in the vicinity of the motor controls or may be all through the body.

During the process of getting the thetan out of the body (and remember, this is getting the *preclear* out of *his* body) the thetan is not, repeat *not,* something else or somebody else, but *is* the preclear. And if the preclear doesn't know that this is himself out of his body–and that he is out of his body–he will have to be run on Sub-zero Tone Scale concepts until he can at last accomplish, under an auditor's direction, departure from the body. During processing, it is good process to have the thetan repair any nerve lines or other matters which he finds to be antipathetic to him in the body.

The rehabilitation of the thetan is up through the Sub-zero range, where beautiful sadness and degradation are the two concepts used, into the band of the plus scale, where beauty and ugliness are used as the feeling.

The feeling differs from the concept and one can have a feeling and a concept at the same time.

An individual who cannot get out of his body immediately can look around inside his head and find the black spots and turn them white, much in the same fashion.*

The technique is simple, but it is most simple to an individual who has a thorough command of the entire subject.

---

*E-therapists and others experimenting with internal awareness occasionally fell accidentally into this manifestation. –LRH*

The rehabilitation of the thetan consists of his being able to sever communications with the body, at will. And consists of making it possible for the thetan not to have a collapsed tractor every time the body is hurt, thus snapping him into the body.

Protection of the body, need of the body, the body getting credit, the feeling that one must have identification, the beautiful sadness of bodies dying are the various concepts which are used in this process.

When the thetan is securely out of the body, he can look around him and find any area of enturbulation and do whatever he pleases about it. He can find vibrations and do what he likes with those.

The sight of a thetan is very bad–as would be the sight of anything below the level of death for the MEST body–and the memory of the thetan for himself is extremely poor. These gradually rehabilitate until the thetan can perceive and recall as himself. His rehabilitation consists mainly of changing his own postulate, rather than running facsimiles.

Wherever possible, avoid running any emotion or effort with the thetan beyond sympathy and those indicated above. These are low-scale manifestations and will fall away.

It is possible for the thetan to pick up whole packages of facsimiles and throw them away at will.

The test of this technique is that in from two to twenty-five hours of processing, an individual can expect to be far above the level of MEST Clear.

The true knowingness and the true beingness of Homo sapiens is his life source. In almost all persons to be processed, it will be discovered that this life source is in very poor condition.

If any difficulties are discovered in utilizing this process, it is recommended that one contact an Associate School of the Hubbard Association of Scientologists.*

Care should be utilized in picking up the areas inside the body which have built up energy on them. This energy is actually the thetan's own energy. It is in ridges. It has individualities because the ridges, being covered with facsimiles, seem to be able to think. And when they are pulled away too rapidly, terrible somatics can result. *Some* somatics can be *expected* to result.

A Theta Clear is one who can get in and out of his body at will. A Cleared Theta Clear is one who has full recall of everything and full ability as a thetan.

---

*See *Addresses* at the back of this book for current locations.

# APPENDIX

# *F*URTHER STUDY
## BOOKS & LECTURES BY L. RON HUBBARD

The materials of Dianetics and Scientology comprise the largest body of information ever assembled on the mind, spirit and life, rigorously refined and codified by L. Ron Hubbard through five decades of research, investigation and development. The results of that work are contained in hundreds of books and more than 3,000 recorded lectures. A full listing and description of them all can be obtained from any Scientology Church or Publications Organization. (See *Guide to the Materials*.)

The books and lectures below form the foundation upon which the Bridge to Freedom is built. They are listed in the sequence Ron wrote or delivered them. In many instances, Ron gave a series of lectures immediately following the release of a new book to provide further explanation and insight of these milestones. Through monumental restoration efforts, those lectures are now available and are listed herein with their companion book.

While Ron's books contain the summaries of breakthroughs and conclusions as they appeared in the developmental research track, his lectures provide the running day-to-day record of research and explain the thoughts, conclusions, tests and demonstrations that lay along that route. In that regard, they are the complete record of the entire research track, providing not only the most important breakthroughs in Man's history, but the *why* and *how* Ron arrived at them.

Not the least advantage of a chronological study of these books and lectures is the inclusion of words and terms which, when originally used, were defined by LRH with considerable exactitude. Far beyond a mere "definition," entire lectures are devoted to a full description of each new Dianetic or Scientology term–what made the breakthrough possible, its application in auditing as well as its application to life itself. As a result, one leaves behind no misunderstoods, obtains a full conceptual understanding of Dianetics and Scientology and grasps the subjects at a level not otherwise possible.

Through a sequential study, you can see how the subject progressed and recognize the highest levels of development. The listing of books and lectures below shows where *Scientology 8-80* fits within the developmental line. From there you can determine your *next* step or any earlier books and lectures you may have missed. You will then be able to fill in missing gaps, not only gaining knowledge of each breakthrough, but greater understanding of what you've already studied.

This is the path to knowing how to know, unlocking the gates to your future eternity. Follow it.

# SCIENTOLOGY 8-80
## L. RON HUBBARD

---

DIANETICS: THE ORIGINAL THESIS • Ron's *first* description of Dianetics. Originally circulated in manuscript form, it was soon copied and passed from hand to hand. Ensuing word of mouth created such demand for more information, Ron concluded the only way to answer the inquiries was with a book. That book was Dianetics: The Modern Science of Mental Health, now the all-time self-help bestseller. Find out what started it all. For here is the bedrock foundation of Dianetic discoveries: the *Original Axioms,* the *Dynamic Principle of Existence,* the *Anatomy of the Analytical* and *Reactive Mind,* the *Dynamics,* the *Tone Scale,* the *Auditor's Code* and the first description of a *Clear.* Even more than that, here are the primary laws describing *how* and *why* auditing works. It's only here in Dianetics: The Original Thesis.

---

DIANETICS: THE EVOLUTION OF A SCIENCE • This is the story of *how* Ron discovered the reactive mind and developed the procedures to get rid of it. Originally written for a national magazine–published to coincide with the release of Dianetics: The Modern Science of Mental Health–it started a wildfire movement virtually overnight upon that book's publication. Here then are both the fundamentals of Dianetics as well as the only account of Ron's two-decade journey of discovery and how he applied a scientific methodology to the problems of the human mind. He wrote it so you would know. Hence, this book is a must for every Dianeticist and Scientologist.

---

DIANETICS: THE MODERN SCIENCE OF MENTAL HEALTH • The bolt from the blue that began a worldwide movement. For while Ron had previously announced his discovery of the reactive mind, it had only fueled the fire of those wanting more information. More to the point–it was humanly impossible for one man to clear an entire planet. Encompassing all his previous discoveries and case histories of those breakthroughs in application, Ron provided the complete handbook of Dianetics procedure to train auditors to use it everywhere. A bestseller for more than half a century and with tens of millions of copies in print, Dianetics: The Modern Science of Mental Health has been translated in more than fifty languages, and used in more than 100 countries of Earth–indisputably, the most widely read and influential book about the human mind ever written. And that is why it will forever be known as *Book One.*

> DIANETICS LECTURES AND DEMONSTRATIONS • Immediately following the publication of *Dianetics,* LRH began lecturing to packed auditoriums across America. Although addressing thousands at a time, demand continued to grow. To meet that demand, his presentation in Oakland, California, was recorded. In these four lectures, Ron related the events that sparked his investigation and his personal journey to his groundbreaking discoveries. He followed it all with a personal demonstration of Dianetics auditing–the only such demonstration of Book One available. *4 lectures.*

# FURTHER STUDY

**DIANETICS PROFESSIONAL COURSE LECTURES–*A SPECIAL COURSE FOR BOOK ONE AUDITORS*** • Following six months of coast-to-coast travel, lecturing to the first Dianeticists, Ron assembled auditors in Los Angeles for a new Professional Course. The subject was his next sweeping discovery on life–the *ARC Triangle,* describing the interrelationship of *Affinity, Reality* and *Communication.* Through a series of fifteen lectures, LRH announced many firsts, including the *Spectrum of Logic,* containing an infinity of gradients from right to wrong; *ARC and the Dynamics;* the *Tone Scales of ARC;* the *Auditor's Code* and how it relates to ARC; and the *Accessibility Chart* that classifies a case and how to process it. Here, then, is both the final statement on Book One Auditing Procedures and the discovery upon which all further research would advance. The data in these lectures was thought to be lost for over fifty years and only available in student notes published in Notes on the Lectures. The original recordings have now been discovered making them broadly available for the first time. Life in its highest state, *Understanding,* is composed of Affinity, Reality and Communication. And, as LRH said, the best description of the ARC Triangle to be found anywhere is in these lectures. *15 lectures.*

---

SCIENCE OF SURVIVAL–*PREDICTION OF HUMAN BEHAVIOR* • The most useful book you will ever own. Built around the *Hubbard Chart of Human Evaluation,* Science of Survival provides the first accurate prediction of human behavior. Included on the chart are all the manifestations of an individual's survival potential graduated from highest to lowest, making this the complete book on the Tone Scale. Knowing only one or two characteristics of a person and using this chart, you can plot his or her position on the Tone Scale and thereby know the rest, obtaining an accurate index of their *entire* personality, conduct and character. Before this book the world was convinced that cases could not improve but only deteriorate. Science of Survival presents the idea of different states of case and the brand-new idea that one can progress upward on the Tone Scale. And therein lies the basis of today's Grade Chart.

**THE SCIENCE OF SURVIVAL LECTURES** • Underlying the development of the Tone Scale and Chart of Human Evaluation was a monumental breakthrough: The *Theta-MEST Theory,* containing the explanation of the interaction between Life–*theta*–with the physical universe of Matter, Energy, Space and Time–*MEST.* In these lectures, delivered to students immediately following publication of the book, Ron gave the most expansive description of all that lies behind the Chart of Human Evaluation and its application in life itself. Moreover, here also is the explanation of how the ratio of *theta* and *en(turbulated)-theta* determines one's position on the Tone Scale and the means to ascend to higher states. *4 lectures.*

# SCIENTOLOGY 8-80
## L. RON HUBBARD

---

SELF ANALYSIS • The barriers of life are really just shadows. Learn to know yourself–not just a shadow of yourself. Containing the most complete description of consciousness, Self Analysis takes you through your past, through your potentials, your life. First, with a series of self-examinations and using a special version of the Hubbard Chart of Human Evaluation, you plot yourself on the Tone Scale. Then, applying a series of light yet powerful processes, you embark on the great adventure of self-discovery. This book further contains embracive principles that reach *any* case, from the lowest to the highest–including auditing techniques so effective they are referred to by Ron again and again through all following years of research into the highest states. In sum, this book not only moves one up the Tone Scale but can pull a person out of almost anything.

---

ADVANCED PROCEDURE AND AXIOMS • With new breakthroughs on the nature and anatomy of engrams–"Engrams are effective only when the individual himself determines that they will be effective"–came the discovery of the being's use of a *Service Facsimile:* a mechanism employed to explain away failures in life, but which then locks a person into detrimental patterns of behavior and further failure. In consequence came a new type of processing addressing *Thought, Emotion* and *Effort* detailed in the "Fifteen Acts" of Advanced Procedure and oriented to the rehabilitation of the preclear's *Self-determinism.* Hence, this book also contains the all-encompassing, no-excuses-allowed explanation of *Full Responsibility,* the key to unlocking it all. Moreover, here is the codification of *Definitions, Logics,* and *Axioms,* providing both the summation of the entire subject and direction for all future research. *See Handbook for Preclears, written as a companion self-processing manual to Advanced Procedure and Axioms.*

THOUGHT, EMOTION AND EFFORT • With the codification of the Axioms came the means to address key points on a case that could unravel all aberration. *Basic Postulates, Prime Thought, Cause and Effect* and their effect on everything from *memory* and *responsibility* to an individual's own role in empowering *engrams*–these matters are only addressed in this series. Here, too, is the most complete description of the *Service Facsimile* found anywhere–and why its resolution removes an individual's self-imposed disabilities. *21 lectures.*

HANDBOOK FOR PRECLEARS • The "Fifteen Acts" of Advanced Procedure and Axioms are paralleled by the fifteen Self-processing Acts given in Handbook for Preclears. Moreover, this book contains several essays giving the most expansive description of the *Ideal State of Man*. Discover why behavior patterns become so solidly fixed; why habits seemingly can't be broken; how decisions long ago have more power over a person than his decisions today; and why a person keeps past negative experiences in the present. It's all clearly laid out on the Chart of Attitudes–a milestone breakthrough that complements the Chart of Human Evaluation–plotting the ideal state of being and one's *attitudes* and *reactions* to life. *In self-processing, Handbook for Preclears is used in conjunction with Self Analysis.*

THE LIFE CONTINUUM • Besieged with requests for lectures on his latest breakthroughs, Ron replied with everything they wanted and more at the Second Annual Conference of Dianetic Auditors. Describing the technology that lies behind the self-processing steps of the *Handbook*–here is the *how* and *why* of it all: the discovery of *Life Continuum*–the mechanism by which an individual is compelled to carry on the life of another deceased or departed individual, generating in his own body the infirmities and mannerisms of the departed. Combined with auditor instruction on use of the Chart of Attitudes in determining how to enter every case at the proper gradient, here, too, are directions for dissemination of the Handbook and hence, the means to begin wide-scale clearing. *10 lectures.*

SCIENTOLOGY: MILESTONE ONE • Ron began the first lecture in this series with six words that would change the world forever: "This is a course in *Scientology*." From there, Ron not only described the vast scope of this, a then brand-new subject, he also detailed his discoveries on past lives. He proceeded from there to the description of the first E-Meter and its initial use in uncovering the *theta line* (the entire track of a thetan's existence), as entirely distinct from the *genetic body line* (the time track of bodies and their physical evolution), shattering the "one-life" lie and revealing the *whole track* of spiritual existence. Here, then, is the very genesis of Scientology. *22 lectures.*

THE ROUTE TO INFINITY: TECHNIQUE 80 LECTURES • As Ron explained, "Technique 80 is the *To Be or Not To Be* Technique." With that, he unveiled the crucial foundation on which ability and sanity rest: *the being's capacity to make a decision*. Here, then, is the anatomy of "maybe," the *Wavelengths of ARC,* the *Tone Scale of Decisions,* and the means to rehabilitate a being's ability *To Be ...* almost *anything. 7 lectures. (Knowledge of Technique 80 is required for Technique 88 as described in Scientology: A History of Man–below.)*

# SCIENTOLOGY 8-80
## L. RON HUBBARD

---

SCIENTOLOGY: A HISTORY OF MAN • "A cold-blooded and factual account of your last 76 trillion years." So begins A History of Man, announcing the revolutionary *Technique 88*–revealing for the first time the truth about whole track experience and the exclusive address, in auditing, to the thetan. Here is history unraveled with the first E-Meter, delineating and describing the principal incidents on the whole track to be found in any human being: *Electronic implants, entities,* the *genetic track, between-lives incidents, how bodies evolved* and *why you got trapped in them*–they're all detailed here.

TECHNIQUE 88: INCIDENTS ON THE TRACK BEFORE EARTH • "Technique 88 is the most hyperbolical, effervescent, dramatic, unexaggeratable, high-flown, superlative, grandiose, colossal and magnificent technique which the mind of Man could conceivably embrace. It is as big as the whole track and all the incidents on it. It's what you apply it to; it's what's been going on. It contains the riddles and secrets, the mysteries of all time. You could bannerline this technique like they do a sideshow, but nothing you could say, no adjective you could use, would adequately describe even a small segment of it. It not only batters the imagination, it makes you ashamed to imagine anything," is Ron's introduction to you in this never-before-available lecture series, expanding on all else contained in History of Man. What awaits you is the whole track itself. *15 lectures.*

---

SCIENTOLOGY 8-80 • *(This current volume.)* The *first* explanation of the electronics of human thought and the energy phenomena in any being. Discover how even physical universe laws of motion are mirrored in a being, not to mention the electronics of aberration. Here is the link between theta and MEST revealing what energy *is,* and how you *create* it. It was this breakthrough that revealed the subject of a thetan's *flows* and which, in turn, is applied in *every* auditing process today. In the book's title, "8-8" stands for *Infinity-Infinity,* and "0" represents the static, *theta.* Included are the *Wavelengths of Emotion, Aesthetics, Beauty and Ugliness, Inflow and Outflow* and the *Sub-zero Tone Scale*–applicable only to the thetan.

SOURCE OF LIFE ENERGY • Beginning with the announcement of his new book–Scientology 8-80–Ron not only unveiled his breakthroughs of theta as the Source of Life Energy, but detailed the *Methods of Research* he used to make that and every other discovery of Dianetics and Scientology: the *Qs* and *Logics*–methods of *thinking* applicable to any universe or thinking process. Here, then, is both *how to think* and *how to evaluate all data and knowledge,* and thus, the linchpin to a full understanding of both Scientology and life itself. *14 lectures.*

# FURTHER STUDY

THE COMMAND OF THETA • While in preparation of his newest book and the Doctorate Course he was about to deliver, Ron called together auditors for a new Professional Course. As he said, "For the first time with this class we are stepping, really, beyond the scope of the word *Survival*." From that vantage point, the Command of Theta gives the technology that bridges the knowledge from 8-80 to 8-8008, and provides the first full explanation of the subject of *Cause* and a permanent shift of orientation in life from MEST to *Theta*. *10 lectures.*

---

SCIENTOLOGY 8-8008 • The complete description of the behavior and potentials of a *thetan*, and textbook for the Philadelphia Doctorate Course and The Factors: Admiration and the Renaissance of Beingness lectures. As Ron said, the book's title serves to fix in the mind of the individual a route by which he can rehabilitate himself, his abilities, his ethics and his goals–the attainment of *infinity* (8) by the reduction of the apparent *infinity* (8) of the MEST universe to *zero* (0) and the increase of the apparent *zero* (0) of one's own universe to *infinity* (8). Condensed herein are more than 80,000 hours of investigation, with a summarization and amplification of every breakthrough to date–and the full significance of those discoveries form the new vantage point of *Operating Thetan*.

THE PHILADELPHIA DOCTORATE COURSE LECTURES • This renowned series stands as the largest single body of work on the anatomy, behavior and potentials of the spirit of Man ever assembled, providing the very fundamentals which underlie the route to Operating Thetan. Here it is in complete detail–the thetan's relationship to the *creation, maintenance* and *destruction of universes*. In just those terms, here is the *anatomy* of matter, energy, space and time, and *postulating* universes into existence. Here, too, is the thetan's fall from whole track abilities and the *universal laws* by which they are restored. In short, here is Ron's codification of the upper echelon of theta beingness and behavior. Lecture after lecture fully expands every concept of the course text, Scientology 8-8008, providing the total scope of *you* in native state. *76 lectures and accompanying reproductions of the original 54 LRH hand-drawn lecture charts.*

THE FACTORS: ADMIRATION AND THE RENAISSANCE OF BEINGNESS • With the *potentials* of a thetan fully established came a look outward resulting in Ron's monumental discovery of a *universal solvent* and the basic laws of the theta *universe*–laws quite literally senior to anything: *The Factors: Summation of the Considerations of the Human Spirit and Material Universe.* So dramatic were these breakthroughs, Ron expanded the book Scientology 8-8008, both clarifying previous discoveries and adding chapter after chapter which, studied with these lectures, provide a postgraduate level to the Doctorate Course. Here then are lectures containing the knowledge of *universal truth* unlocking the riddle of creation itself. *18 lectures.*

THE CREATION OF HUMAN ABILITY–*A HANDBOOK FOR SCIENTOLOGISTS* •
On the heels of his discoveries of Operating Thetan came a year of intensive research,
exploring the realm of a *thetan exterior.* Through auditing and instruction, including
450 lectures in this same twelve-month span, Ron codified the entire subject of
Scientology. And it's all contained in this handbook, from a *Summary of Scientology*
to its basic *Axioms* and *Codes.* Moreover, here is *Intensive Procedure,* containing
the famed Exteriorization Processes of *Route 1* and *Route 2*–processes drawn right
from the Axioms. Each one is described in detail–*how* the process is used, *why* it
works, the axiomatic technology that underlies its use, and the complete explanation
of how a being can break the *false agreements* and *self-created barriers* that enslave
him to the physical universe. In short, this book contains the ultimate summary of
thetan exterior OT ability and its permanent accomplishment.

PHOENIX LECTURES: FREEING THE HUMAN SPIRIT • Here is the
panoramic view of Scientology complete. Having codified the subject
of Scientology in Creation of Human Ability, Ron then delivered a series of
half-hour lectures to specifically accompany a full study of the book. From the
*essentials* that underlie the technology–*The Axioms, Conditions of Existence*
and *Considerations and Mechanics,* to the processes of *Intensive Procedure,*
including twelve lectures describing one-by-one the thetan exterior processes
of *Route 1*–it's all covered in full, providing a conceptual understanding
of the *science of knowledge* and *native state OT ability.* Here then are the
bedrock principles upon which everything in Scientology rests, including the
embracive statement of the religion and its heritage–*Scientology, Its General
Background.* Hence, this is the watershed lecture series on Scientology itself,
and the axiomatic foundation for all future research. *42 lectures.*

DIANETICS 55!–*THE COMPLETE MANUAL OF HUMAN COMMUNICATION* •
With all breakthroughs to date, a single factor had been isolated as crucial to success
in every type of auditing. As LRH said, "Communication is so thoroughly important
today in Dianetics and Scientology (as it always has been on the whole track) that it
could be said if you were to get a preclear into communication, you would get him
well." And this book delineates the *exact,* but previously unknown, anatomy and
formulas for *perfect* communication. The magic of the communication cycle is *the*
fundamental of auditing and the primary reason auditing works. The breakthroughs
here opened new vistas of application–discoveries of such magnitude, LRH called
Dianetics 55! the *Second Book* of Dianetics.

THE UNIFICATION CONGRESS: COMMUNICATION! FREEDOM &
ABILITY • The historic Congress announcing the reunification of the
subjects of Dianetics and Scientology with the release of *Dianetics 55!* Until
now, each had operated in their own sphere: Dianetics addressed Man *as
Man*–the first four dynamics, while Scientology addressed *life itself*–the Fifth
to Eighth Dynamics. The formula which would serve as the foundation for
all future development was contained in a single word: *Communication.* It
was a paramount breakthrough Ron would later call, "the great discovery
of Dianetics and Scientology." Here, then, are the lectures, as it happened.
*16 lectures and accompanying reproductions of the original LRH hand-drawn
lecture charts.*

# FURTHER
# STUDY

SCIENTOLOGY: THE FUNDAMENTALS OF THOUGHT–*THE BASIC BOOK OF THE THEORY AND PRACTICE OF SCIENTOLOGY FOR BEGINNERS* • Designated by Ron as the *Book One of Scientology.* After having fully unified and codified the subjects of Dianetics and Scientology came the refinement of their *fundamentals.* Originally published as a résumé of Scientology for use in translations into non-English tongues, this book is of inestimable value to both the beginner and advanced student of the mind, spirit and life. Equipped with this book alone, one can begin a practice and perform seeming miracle changes in the states of well-being, ability and intelligence of people. Contained within are the *Conditions of Existence, Eight Dynamics, ARC Triangle, Parts of Man,* the full analysis of *Life as a Game,* and more, including exact processes for individual application of these principles in processing. Here, then, in one book, is the starting point for bringing Scientology to people everywhere.

HUBBARD PROFESSIONAL COURSE LECTURES • While Fundamentals of Thought stands as an introduction to the subject for beginners, it also contains a distillation of fundamentals for every Scientologist. Here are the in-depth descriptions of those fundamentals, each lecture one-half hour in length and providing, one-by-one, a complete mastery of a single Scientology breakthrough–*Axioms 1-10; The Anatomy of Control; Handling of Problems; Start, Change and Stop; Confusion and Stable Data; Exteriorization; Valences* and more–the *why* behind them, *how* they came to be and their mechanics. And it's all brought together with the *Code of a Scientologist,* point by point, and its use in actually creating a new civilization. In short, here are the LRH lectures that make a *Professional Scientologist*–one who can apply the subject to every aspect of life. *21 lectures.*

# ADDITIONAL BOOKS CONTAINING SCIENTOLOGY ESSENTIALS

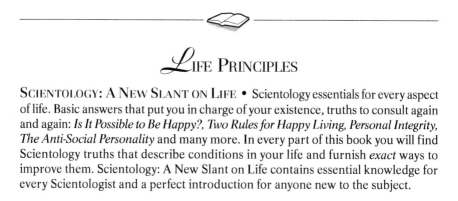

## WORK

THE PROBLEMS OF WORK–*SCIENTOLOGY APPLIED TO THE WORKADAY WORLD* • Having codified the entire subject of Scientology, Ron immediately set out to provide the *beginning* manual for its application by anyone. As he described it: life is composed of seven-tenths work, one-tenth familial, one-tenth political and one-tenth relaxation. Here, then, is Scientology applied to that seven-tenths of existence including the answers to *Exhaustion* and the *Secret of Efficiency*. Here, too, is the analysis of life itself–a game composed of exact rules. Know them and you succeed. Problems of Work contains technology no one can live without, and that can immediately be applied by both the Scientologist and those new to the subject.

## LIFE PRINCIPLES

SCIENTOLOGY: A NEW SLANT ON LIFE • Scientology essentials for every aspect of life. Basic answers that put you in charge of your existence, truths to consult again and again: *Is It Possible to Be Happy?, Two Rules for Happy Living, Personal Integrity, The Anti-Social Personality* and many more. In every part of this book you will find Scientology truths that describe conditions in your life and furnish *exact* ways to improve them. Scientology: A New Slant on Life contains essential knowledge for every Scientologist and a perfect introduction for anyone new to the subject.

## AXIOMS, CODES AND SCALES

SCIENTOLOGY 0-8: THE BOOK OF BASICS • The companion to *all* Ron's books, lectures and materials. This is *the* Book of Basics, containing indispensable data you will refer to constantly: the *Axioms of Dianetics and Scientology; The Factors;* a full compilation of all *Scales*–more than 100 in all; listings of the *Perceptics* and *Awareness Levels;* all *Codes* and *Creeds* and much more. The senior laws of existence are condensed into this single volume, distilled from more than **15,000** pages of writings, **3,000** lectures and scores of books.

# $\mathcal{S}$CIENTOLOGY ETHICS:
## TECHNOLOGY OF OPTIMUM SURVIVAL

INTRODUCTION TO SCIENTOLOGY ETHICS • A new hope for Man arises with the first workable technology of ethics–technology to help an individual pull himself out of the downward skid of life and to a higher plateau of survival. This is the comprehensive handbook providing the crucial fundamentals: *Basics of Ethics & Justice; Honesty; Conditions of Existence; Condition Formulas* from Confusion to Power; the *Basics of Suppression* and its handling; as well as *Justice Procedures* and their use in Scientology Churches. Here, then, is the technology to overcome any barriers in life and in one's personal journey up the Bridge to Total Freedom.

# $\mathcal{P}$URIFICATION

CLEAR BODY, CLEAR MIND–*THE EFFECTIVE PURIFICATION PROGRAM* • We live in a biochemical world, and this book is the solution. While investigating the harmful effects that earlier drug use had on preclears' cases, Ron made the major discovery that many street drugs, particularly LSD, remained in a person's body long after ingested. Residues of the drug, he noted, could have serious and lasting effects, including triggering further "trips." Additional research revealed that a wide range of substances–medical drugs, alcohol, pollutants, household chemicals and even food preservatives–could also lodge in the body's tissues. Through research on thousands of cases, he developed the *Purification Program* to eliminate their destructive effects. Clear Body, Clear Mind details every aspect of the all-natural regimen that can free one from the harmful effects of drugs and other toxins, opening the way for spiritual progress.

# ℛEFERENCE HANDBOOKS

## WHAT IS SCIENTOLOGY?

𝒯he complete and essential encyclopedic reference on the subject and practice of Scientology. Organized for use, this book contains the pertinent data on every aspect of the subject:

• The life of L. Ron Hubbard and his path of discovery

• The Spiritual Heritage of the religion

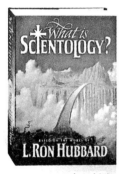

• A full description of Dianetics and Scientology

• Auditing–what it is and how it works

• Courses–what they contain and how they are structured

• The Grade Chart of Services and how one ascends to higher states

• The Scientology Ethics and Justice System

• The Organizational Structure of the Church

• A complete description of the many Social Betterment programs supported by the Church, including: Drug Rehabilitation, Criminal Reform, Literacy and Education and the instilling of real values for morality

Over 1,000 pages in length, with more than 500 photographs and illustrations, this text further includes Creeds, Codes, a full listing of all books and materials as well as a Catechism with answers to virtually any question regarding the subject.

*You Ask and This Book Answers.*

## THE SCIENTOLOGY HANDBOOK

𝒮cientology fundamentals for daily use in every part of life. Encompassing 19 separate bodies of technology, here is the most comprehensive manual on the basics of life ever published. Each chapter contains key principles and technology for your continual use:

• Study Technology

• The Dynamics of Existence

• The Components of Understanding– Affinity, Reality and Communication

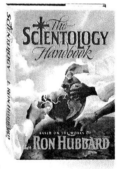

• The Tone Scale

• Communication and its Formulas

• Assists for Illnesses and Injuries

• How to Resolve Conflicts

• Integrity and Honesty

• Ethics and Condition Formulas

• Answers to Suppression and a Dangerous Environment

• Marriage

• Children

• Tools for the Workplace

More than 700 photographs and illustrations make it easy for you to learn the procedures and apply them at once. This book is truly the indispensable handbook for every Scientologist.

*The Technology to Build a Better World.*

# About L. Ron Hubbard

"To really know life," L. Ron Hubbard wrote, "you've got to be part of life. You must get down and look, you must get into the nooks and crannies of existence. You have to rub elbows with all kinds and types of men before you can finally establish what he is."

Through his long and extraordinary journey to the founding of Dianetics and Scientology, Ron did just that. From his adventurous youth in a rough and tumble American West to his far-flung trek across a still mysterious Asia; from his two-decade search for the very essence of life to the triumph of Dianetics and Scientology—such are the stories recounted in the L. Ron Hubbard Biographical Publications.

Presenting the photographic overview of Ron's greater journey is *L. Ron Hubbard: Images of a Lifetime*. Drawn from his own archival collection, this is Ron's life as he himself saw it.

While for the many aspects of that rich and varied life, stands the Ron Series. Each issue focuses on a specific LRH profession: *Auditor, Humanitarian, Philosopher, Artist, Poet, Music Maker, Photographer* and many more including his published articles on *Freedom* and his personal *Letters & Journals*. Here is the life of a man who lived at least twenty lives in the space of one.

## For Further Information Visit
### www.lronhubbard.org

# GUIDE TO THE MATERIALS

## YOU'RE ON AN ADVENTURE!
## HERE'S THE MAP.

- All books
- All lectures
- All reference books

All of it laid out in chronological sequence with descriptions of what each contains.

*Y*our journey to a full understanding of Dianetics and Scientology is the greatest adventure of all. But you need a map that shows you where you are and where you are going.

That map is the Materials Guide Chart. It shows all Ron's books and lectures with a full description of their content and subject matter so you can find exactly what *you* are looking for and precisely what *you* need.

Since each book and lecture is laid out in chronological sequence, you can see *how* the subjects of Dianetics and Scientology were developed. And what that means is by simply studying this chart you are in for cognition after cognition!

New editions of all books include extensive glossaries, containing definitions for every technical term. And as a result of a monumental restoration program, the entire library of Ron's lectures are being made available on compact disc, with complete transcripts, glossaries, lecture graphs, diagrams and issues he refers to in the lectures. As a result, you get *all* the data, and can learn with ease, gaining a full *conceptual* understanding.

And what that adds up to is a new Golden Age of Knowledge every Dianeticist and Scientologist has dreamed of.

**To obtain your FREE Materials Guide Chart and Catalog, or to order L. Ron Hubbard's books and lectures, contact:**

WESTERN HEMISPHERE:
**Bridge
Publications, Inc.**
4751 Fountain Avenue
Los Angeles, CA 90029 USA
**www.bridgepub.com**
Phone: 1-800-722-1733
Fax: 1-323-953-3328

EASTERN HEMISPHERE:
**New Era Publications
International ApS**
Store Kongensgade 53
1264 Copenhagen K, Denmark
**www.newerapublications.com**
Phone: (45) 33 73 66 66
Fax: (45) 33 73 66 33

*Books and lectures are also available direct from Churches of Scientology.*
*See Addresses.*

# DDRESSES

$\mathscr{S}$ cientology is the fastest-growing religion in the world today. Churches and Missions exist in cities throughout the world, and new ones are continually forming.

To obtain more information or to locate the Church nearest you, visit the Scientology website:

**www.scientology.org**
**e-mail: info@scientology.org**

or

**Phone: 1-800-334-LIFE**
**(for US and Canada)**

You can also write to any one of the Continental Organizations, listed on the following page, who can direct you to one of the thousands of Churches and Missions world over.

L. Ron Hubbard's books and lectures may be obtained from any of these addresses or direct from the publishers on the previous page.

# CONTINENTAL CHURCH ORGANIZATIONS:

## UNITED STATES

CHURCH OF SCIENTOLOGY
CONTINENTAL LIAISON OFFICE
WESTERN UNITED STATES
1308 L. Ron Hubbard Way
Los Angeles, California 90027 USA
info@wus.scientology.org

CHURCH OF SCIENTOLOGY
CONTINENTAL LIAISON OFFICE
EASTERN UNITED STATES
349 W. 48th Street
New York, New York 10036 USA
info@eus.scientology.org

## CANADA

CHURCH OF SCIENTOLOGY
CONTINENTAL LIAISON OFFICE
CANADA
696 Yonge Street, 2nd Floor
Toronto, Ontario
Canada M4Y 2A7
info@scientology.ca

## LATIN AMERICA

CHURCH OF SCIENTOLOGY
CONTINENTAL LIAISON OFFICE
LATIN AMERICA
Federacion Mexicana de Dianetica
Calle Puebla #31
Colonia Roma, Mexico D.F.
C.P. 06700, Mexico
info@scientology.org.mx

## UNITED KINGDOM

CHURCH OF SCIENTOLOGY
CONTINENTAL LIAISON OFFICE
UNITED KINGDOM
Saint Hill Manor
East Grinstead, West Sussex
England, RH19 4JY
info@scientology.org.uk

## AFRICA

CHURCH OF SCIENTOLOGY
CONTINENTAL LIAISON OFFICE AFRICA
5 Cynthia Street
Kensington
Johannesburg 2094, South Africa
info@scientology.org.za

## AUSTRALIA, NEW ZEALAND & OCEANIA
**CHURCH OF SCIENTOLOGY
CONTINENTAL LIAISON OFFICE ANZO**
16 Dorahy Street
Dundas, New South Wales 2117
Australia
info@scientology.org.au

> **Church of Scientology
> Liaison Office of Taiwan**
> 1st, No. 231, Cisian 2nd Road
> Kaoshiung City
> Taiwan, ROC
> info@scientology.org.tw

## EUROPE
**CHURCH OF SCIENTOLOGY
CONTINENTAL LIAISON OFFICE EUROPE**
Store Kongensgade 55
1264 Copenhagen K, Denmark
info@scientology.org.dk

> **Church of Scientology
> Liaison Office of Commonwealth
> of Independent States**
> Management Center of Dianetics
> and Scientology Dissemination
> Pervomajskaya Street, House 1A
> Korpus Grazhdanskoy Oboroni
> Losino-Petrovsky Town
> 141150 Moscow, Russia
> info@scientology.ru

> **Church of Scientology
> Liaison Office of Central Europe**
> 1082 Leonardo da Vinci u. 8-14
> Budapest, Hungary
> info@scientology.hu

> **Church of Scientology
> Liaison Office of Iberia**
> C/Miguel Menendez Boneta, 18
> 28460 - Los Molinos
> Madrid, Spain
> info@spain.scientology.org

> **Church of Scientology
> Liaison Office of Italy**
> Via Cadorna, 61
> 20090 Vimodrone
> Milan, Italy
> info@scientology.it

140

# ℬECOME A MEMBER
## OF THE INTERNATIONAL
## ASSOCIATION OF SCIENTOLOGISTS

The International Association of Scientologists is the membership organization of all Scientologists united in the most vital crusade on Earth.

A free Six-Month Introductory Membership is extended to anyone who has not held a membership with the Association before.

As a member, you are eligible for discounts on Scientology materials offered only to IAS Members. You also receive the Association magazine, *IMPACT,* issued six times a year, full of Scientology news from around the world.

The purpose of the IAS is:

*"To unite, advance, support and protect Scientology and Scientologists in all parts of the world so as to achieve the Aims of Scientology as originated by L. Ron Hubbard."*

Join the strongest force for positive change on the planet today, opening the lives of millions to the greater truth embodied in Scientology.

### JOIN THE INTERNATIONAL
### ASSOCIATION OF SCIENTOLOGISTS.

To apply for membership,
write to the International
Association of Scientologists
c/o Saint Hill Manor, East Grinstead
West Sussex, England, RH19 4JY

**www.iasmembership.org**

# EDITOR'S GLOSSARY
## OF WORDS, TERMS & PHRASES

*Words often have several meanings. The definitions used here only give the meaning that the word has as it is used in this book. Dianetics and Scientology terms appear in bold type. Beside each definition you will find the page on which it first appears, so you can refer back to the text if you wish.*

*This glossary is not meant to take the place of standard language or Dianetics and Scientology dictionaries, which should be referred to for any words, terms or phrases that do not appear below.*

*– The Editors*

- • (dot): a symbol for multiplication. For example: $3 \cdot 3 = 9$. Title page.

- ∞ (infinity): the condition of being unable to be measured; the state or quality of being infinite, having no limit or end. Page 22.

- (-f) parentheses: both of a pair of the upright curved lines ( ) used in a mathematical expression to sometimes mark off a number or quantity that is to be multiplied by another number or quantity. For example, in multiplying 3 times 3 one can write either $3 \cdot 3$ or $(3) \cdot (3)$. The dot between the two 3s is a symbol for multiplication. Title page.

**aberree:** an aberrated person. Page 24.

AC: an abbreviation for *alternating current,* electricity that flows for only a short while in one direction and then reverses to flow a short while in the opposite direction (as opposed to direct current, as in a battery). It keeps reversing or alternating back and forth at a rapid rate. For example, most electrical outlets operate on alternating current. Page 67.

**according:** agreeing in nature or action; in harmony. Page 103.

**according to:** 1. on the authority of; as stated by. Page 9.

2. in a manner consistent or agreeing with something else. Page 91.

**after all:** everything else having been considered (used when explaining something or when giving a reason for something). Page 9.

**agitation:** the action or process of moving or forcing into violent, irregular action. Page 98.

**all but:** almost; very nearly. Page 15.

**all of his own:** completely independent of outside help or influence. Page 5.

**alternating current:** electricity that flows for only a short while in one direction and then reverses to flow a short while in the opposite direction (as opposed to direct current, as in a battery). It keeps reversing or alternating back and forth at a rapid rate. For example, most electrical outlets operate on alternating current. Page 67.

**antipathetic:** having a feeling of *antipathy,* an instinctive opposition or hostility, to something that one considers disagreeable, offensive or the like; strong or deep-rooted dislike. Page 117.

**appended:** attached to something. Page 24.

**as if:** used to emphasize that something is not the case and is even ridiculous. Page 43.

**Associate School:** a school affiliated with the Hubbard College in Phoenix, Arizona, 1952. The Hubbard College, where auditors trained on professional courses, had some twelve associates throughout the country. Each one of them had its own professional courses, played lecture tapes, gave professional processing and distributed books. See *Addresses* for current locations. Page 119.

**at length:** after some time; eventually. Page 17.

**atom bomb:** short for *atomic bomb,* an extremely destructive type of bomb, the power of which results from the immense quantity of energy suddenly released with the splitting of the nuclei (centers) of atoms into fragments. Page 102.

**attention units:** energy flows of small wavelengths and definite frequency; quantities of awareness. Page 16.

**automaton:** a human being acting mechanically or without active intelligence in a monotonous routine; a robot. Page 101.

**Axioms:** the Dianetic Axioms, statements of natural laws on the order of those of the physical sciences. Page 9.

**band:** a more or less well-defined range of something, as a level on a scale. Page 31.

**basic:** something that is fundamental; an essential ingredient. Page 9.

**basic facsimile:** the earliest facsimile on a chain. Page 23.

**bear upon:** to be a problem for or a burden to; cause difficulty to. Page 11.

**beat (someone) into:** apply forceful means (such as by blows) to someone in an attempt to cause them to do or be something. Page 24.

**beautiful sadness:** there are two classes of Aesthetic Running. There is the "beauty," which is upper scale with "ugliness." And there's "beautiful sadness" which is lower scale. Page 80.

**be other than:** (usually used in negative statements) be different than something else. Page 30.

**better, for the:** in a way that improves a person, situation, condition, etc. Page 16.

**better, had:** ought to or must do something; would find it wiser, as in *"Thus we had better know what makes a facsimile 'hang up.'"* Page 16.

**better to ____, the:** so as to do the specified thing more effectively. Page 43.

**bitterest:** characterized by the strongest feelings of hatred, resentment or the like. Page 30.

**Blanketings:** incidents where thetans throw themselves over another thetan or MEST body to obtain an emotional impact or even to kill. This is basic on fastening on to a MEST body or holding a MEST body or protecting MEST bodies. Blanketings are described in *Scientology: A History of Man*. Page 59.

**blazing:** burning brightly and with great force; of tremendous intensity or fervor. Page 69.

**blazing and crackling:** refers to the look and sound one can observe near some high-powered electrical lines. *See also* **blazing** as well as **crackling**. Page 69.

**blow out:** cause something to (suddenly) dissipate and disappear as if by explosion. Page 110.

**boil:** short for *boil-off,* the manifestation of former periods of unconsciousness, accompanied by grogginess. In its English usage, *boil-off* refers to the reduction of quantity of a liquid by its conversion to a gaseous state, such as steam. Boil-off is described in *Dianetics: The Modern Science of Mental Health*. Page 37.

**boil-off:** the manifestation of former periods of unconsciousness, accompanied by grogginess. In its English usage, *boil-off* refers to the reduction of quantity of a liquid by its conversion to a gaseous state, such as steam. Boil-off is described in *Dianetics: The Modern Science of Mental Health*. Page 37.

**borrowed:** thetans like facsimiles just like a Homo sapiens likes TV. A thetan can take a facsimile and inspect it. He likes to collect them like a bibliophile (a person who loves books) collects books. Any thetan has purloined (stolen; taken for oneself) packages of facsimiles from other thetans just like schoolboys take pictures of champions away from each other. Thus your thetan has two things: he has his own record of real experience of things which actually happened to him and he has whole banks of second facsimiles or "photographs" he has taken from other thetans' banks. These are "borrowed" facsimiles or entire banks. The subject of "borrowing" is described in *Scientology: A History of Man*. Page 17.

**bouncer:** in Dianetics, a *bouncer* is a type of action phrase (words or phrases in engrams or locks which cause the individual to perform involuntary actions on the time track). A bouncer ejects the preclear from an incident and up the track toward present time. ("Get up," "Get out," "I've got to get ahead," etc.) The subject of bouncers is described in *Dianetics: The Modern Science of Mental Health*. Page 86.

**bouncing:** causing to be forcibly ejected or expelled. *Bounce* literally means to spring back from something. Hence, *"When the preclear cannot get the field, an electronic flow is bouncing him."* See **bouncer** in this glossary for context of the word's use and meaning in Dianetics. Page 37.

**bounds of, within the:** inside the boundaries of something, as if lying within a particular region or sphere of activity that is marked or set apart from others. Page 102.

**brought into play:** put into operation or motion; caused to come into force or activity. Page 11.

**built down:** reduced or diminished. Page 23.

**bully:** intimidate (use force on or threaten) or mistreat. Page 5.

**capping beam:** beams the thetan uses to put an electronic cap over the genetic entity in the body, squelching it and taking it over. (*Squelching* means suppressing or silencing someone as if by a forceful blow.) Page 110.

**carbon batteries:** batteries that utilize carbon as one of their components to produce electricity. A carbon battery consists of two different terminals: one is positive (made of carbon) and the other negative (made of zinc), the difference causing an electrical flow. Page 66.

**cellular:** having to do with a *cell,* the smallest structural unit of an organism that is capable of independent functioning. All plants and animals are made up materially of one or more cells that usually combine to form various tissues. For instance the human body has more than 10 trillion cells. Page 66.

**centimeter:** one hundredth of a meter (a meter is 39.4 inches). Page 21.

**chain fission:** used in this book as an analogy to the chain reaction that takes place when the center portion of an atom (nucleus) is split (fissioned) into smaller parts, with these smaller parts ejecting outward and splitting other atoms, which in turn split others and so on. Page 67.

**Chart of Attitudes:** a chart which notes the ideal state of being and one's attitudes and reactions in life. The Chart of Attitudes is contained in *Handbook for Preclears.* Page 47.

**circuit:** a pseudopersonality out of a facsimile strong enough to dictate to the individual and BE the individual. For a full explanation of circuits, see *Dianetics: The Modern Science of Mental Health.* Page 109.

**Clear, MEST:** an individual who no longer retains engrams or locks. Page 30.

**Clear, Theta:** a person who can get in and out of his body at will. Page 59.

**cm:** a symbol for *centimeter,* one hundredth of a meter (a meter is 39.4 inches). Page 22.

**coarse:** lacking in fineness, smoothness or delicacy, as of shape, structure or the like; consisting of individual parts or sections that are relatively large. Page 24.

**come about:** take place or occur; happen. Page 16.

**come into play:** come into operation or motion; become active or in force. Page 56.

**communication lines:** the thetan uses tractor beams to take perceptions out of the body. So he lifts out of the channels of the body. Almost any place there is a ridge, he'll put a little tractor there. And he'll build up standard channels and then let them hang. Furthermore, early on the track, he customarily wanted bodies to want something from him, so he put reverse tractors onto the body. So you've got all these various combinations of tractors and they build up an enormous complexity of ridges. These are communication lines. Even if they're terrible communication lines, they are communication lines. So the thetan leaves them like that. They don't have to be like that at all. The thetan can operate, directly and alively, the body–straight to its motor controls where they are supposed to be. Page 110.

**compulsion:** the state or condition of being compelled (overpowered); an irresistible impulse that is irrational or contrary to one's own will. Page 17.

**concept:** something formed in the mind; a general idea or thought. Page 16.

**Concept Processing:** also called *Concept Running*. Processing where the preclear "gets the idea" of knowing or not being and holds it, the while looking at his time track. The concept runs out or the somatic it brings on runs out and the concept itself is run. It is not addressed at individual incidents but at hundreds. Concept Running is described in Chapter Eight. Page 29.

**Concept Running:** *see* **Concept Processing.**

**concepts, low-scale:** a reference to the Chart of Attitudes which plots the ideal state of being and one's attitudes and reactions in life. "I Am Not" and "I Know Not" are at the bottom of the chart, 0.5, Apathy. See *Handbook for Preclears*. Page 30.

**condenser:** a device for accumulating (from *condensing* which means to make more dense or compact) and holding electrical charge. A condenser consists of two equally but oppositely charged conducting surfaces held apart by insulating material. Page 66.

**conduit:** a channel or medium by which anything is conveyed, such as a pipe or tube protecting electronic wires or cables for telephone lines. Page 102.

**conservation of energy:** a law of physics that states that energy, itself, cannot be created and destroyed but can only alter its forms. For example, if one burned a piece of coal and collected all the smoke, ash and other particles which radiated from the burning and weighed them, one would have the same weight as before the coal was burned. Page 102.

**constant:** something that is invariable and does not change, such as a quantity that always has the same value. Page 99.

**control mechanisms:** means or systems that operate to restrain, regulate or dominate a person, his ideas, emotions, judgment or the like. Page 23.

**conversely:** used to indicate that a situation one is about to describe is the reverse of the one just described. Page 16.

**conviction:** characterized by the power to bring one to a firm belief in the truth or certainty of something. Page 30.

**corbitrons:** a made-up name for particles (very, very small pieces of matter with particular characteristics). Page 100.

**counter:** acting in opposition; lying or tending in the opposite direction; having an opposite tendency, to the opposite effect. Page 86.

counter-elasticity of flow: *see* counter and elasticity. See further text, immediately following this term, which explains the *theory of counter-elasticity of flow.* Page 102.

*(Additional data on this phenomenon may be found in the lecture "Flows" contained in transcript form in the Source of Life Energy lecture series package supplement. Further information can be found in the Research & Discovery volumes containing the Technique 88 Supplementary lecture series–September and October 1952.)*

counterfeit: something that gives a false appearance; an imitation of something genuine that deceives. Page 42.

counterpart: something that is equivalent (has equal value, amount, function, meaning, etc.) and duplicates another thing in characteristics and operation but in a different place or context. Page 23.

course (of something): 1. a systematic or orderly series of steps, as in *"The course of auditing."* Page 94.

2. the continuous passage or progress through time or a succession of stages, as in *"Thus the auditor must not be dismayed at the course of tone, but should simply persevere."* Page 94.

crackling: exhibiting liveliness, vibrancy, etc. Literally, the making of slight cracking sounds rapidly repeated. Page 69.

crests: the tops or highest points of something, such as waves. Page 21.

cut away: take or clear away something as if by separating with a sharp tool; remove by severing. Page 24.

DC: an abbreviation for *direct current,* electricity that flows in only one direction. Flashlight batteries and those used in most portable equipment are examples. Page 67.

DED: *DED* stands for *DEserveD action,* an incident the preclear does to another dynamic and for which he has no motivator–i.e., he punishes or hurts or wrecks something the like of which has never hurt him. Now he must justify the incident. He will use things which didn't happen to him. He claims that the object of his injury really deserved it, hence the word, which is a sarcasm. See *Scientology: A History of Man.* Page 56.

**DEDEX:** an incident which happens to a preclear after he has a DED. It is always on the same chain or subject, is always after the DED. It means the DED EXposed. It is covered guilt. Its effect on the preclear is all out of proportion to the actual injury to him. One would think he was murdered by the harsh word or the scratch. He will explain violently how terribly he has been used. See *Scientology: A History of Man.* Page 56.

**demon circuits of the mind:** in Dianetics, a "demon" is a parasitic circuit. It has an action in the mind which approximates another entity than self and was considered in Dianetics to be derived entirely from words in engrams. Their phenomena are described in *Dianetics: The Modern Science of Mental Health.* "Demon circuits of the mind" are described in *8-80* as ridges that act like beings when sprayed with energy or when permitted to give off energy. The ridges, being covered with facsimiles, seem to be able to think. Ridges are fully described in Chapters Eighteen and Nineteen. Page 111.

**derangement:** the condition of being out of order, not working. Page 115.

**designate:** to give something a formal description or name. Page 100.

**dichotomy:** opposites or near opposites. Two things which, when interplayed, cause action: God and the Devil, that is a dichotomy–good and evil. If God is just sitting there, good all the time, there is no action. But if good and evil are interplaying, there is lots of action. Opposites don't have to be absolute, like God and the Devil. They can be much closer together and still form a dichotomy so that there can be an interplay. Page 67.

**difference:** the amount by which one quantity differs from another; the remainder left after subtracting one quantity (number) from another. Page 66.

**direct current:** electricity that flows in only one direction. Flashlight batteries and those used in most portable equipment are examples. Page 100.

**Disbelief:** another name for *Distrust,* a button on the Chart of Attitudes. *Distrust* appears in the Faith-Distrust column on the chart and is interchangeable with the term *Disbelief;* that is, the column might also be called the column of Belief-Disbelief. *Disbelief* means the inability or refusal to believe or to accept something as true. Page 30.

**discharging:** a *discharge* is the flow of electricity which takes place between two oppositely charged objects when they touch together, or when a path is provided between the objects for electricity to flow. An example is the spark or jolt that you feel when you touch a doorknob after walking across a carpet on a dry day. A terminal is *discharging* against another terminal when the charge is allowed to flow from one to the other. Page 98.

**discharging condenser:** in an electronic circuit, a condenser (also called a *capacitor*) can accumulate large quantities of energy and when releasing it produce a far greater effect than the electrical flow itself was capable of. *See also* condenser and discharging. Page 66.

**discord:** lack of harmony or agreement. Page 42.

**disharmony:** lack of harmony; in discord. In music, a combination of musical tones that sound disagreeable to the ear or harsh. *See also* harmony. Page 41.

**dismayed:** discouraged or disappointed. Page 94.

**dispersal:** the action of something *dispersing,* moving or scattering out in different directions. Page 55.

**dissipate:** to disperse; to alleviate; to cause to vanish. Page 17.

**Distrust:** a button on the Chart of Attitudes appearing in the Faith–Distrust column. *Distrust* means to regard with doubt or suspicion; have no faith, trust or confidence in. Page 30.

**do:** to be sufficient for some purpose; serve. Page 17.

**dot (•):** a symbol for multiplication. For example: 3•3 = 9. Title page.

**do unto others what was done to you:** a reference to the phrase *do unto others as you would have them do unto you,* meaning do only those things to another as you would have them do to you. This is a principle of conduct found in many religious faiths and races. Page 10.

**do what (one) will:** used to mean that whatever one does, it doesn't matter because the condition or result will be the same. Page 65.

**drop:** literally, cause to sink to a lower position. Hence, to cause to become less in intensity, value, amount, quality, etc. Page 17.

**drop off:** let or make fall (away) as by releasing hold of. Page 25.

**dropping out:** allowing something to fall away, as if by letting go of it. Page 16.

**dub-in:** a term used to characterize vision or recall which is imaginary. The term comes from the motion-picture industry. To "dub," in moviemaking, is to create and add sounds to a picture after filming is complete. This process ("dubbing") results in a fabricated soundtrack that *seems* to the audience like it actually took place when filmed. But in fact, much, or *all* of it, was created in the studio long after filming was finished, and was then "dubbed in." Hence, "dub-in" is something put there that seems like it happened, but in reality it did not. Page 111.

**effort:** the physical-force manifestation of motion. A sharp effort against an individual produces pain. A strenuous effort produces discomfort. Effort can be recalled and re-experienced by the preclear. The essential part of a painful facsimile is its effort, not its perceptions. See *Advanced Procedure and Axioms.* Page 9.

**Effort Processing:** Effort Processing is done by running moments of physical stress. These are run either as simple efforts or counter-efforts or as whole precise incidents. Such incidents as those which contain physical pain or heavy stress of motion, such as injuries, accidents or illnesses, are addressed by *effort.* Effort Processing is described in the book *Advanced Procedure and Axioms* and its companion lecture series *Thought, Emotion and Effort.* Page 29.

**EI:** Energy Potential multiplied by Energy Flow. In mathematics, multiplication can be indicated by putting two letters next to each other (EI) or by a dot between two letters (A·B) or by inserting an "x" between the letters (A x B). Title page.

**elasticity:** the state or quality of being elastic; flexibility. In physics, *elasticity* is the property that enables something to change its length, volume or shape in direct response to a force effecting such a change and to recover its original form upon the removal of the force. An example is a rubber band, that can be stretched out and then when released will snap back to its original size. Many materials can be changed in this way in small amounts, but become permanently deformed if the force is too great. A metal, for example, can be bent to a small degree, then snap back straight again. But if it is bent too far it will stay bent. Page 102.

**electrical field:** a region, volume or space where a specific, measurable electrical influence, force, etc., exists. Page 10.

**electric generator:** a machine or mechanical device which produces electricity. *See also* **generator.** Page 66.

**electric light wire:** a reference to the thin wire in an electric light bulb that heats up and glows (producing the light) when electricity flows through it. Page 97.

**electronic:** an incident of tremendous force, marked by the use of heavy electrical currents. Electronic incidents on the whole track are fully described in *Scientology: A History of Man.* Page 37.

**electronics:** the science dealing with the development and application of devices and systems involving the flow of electrical energy in vacuums, gases and solids. Page 66.

**electrons:** tiny particles of matter that have a negative electrical charge. Page 98.

**encroaching:** intruding or impinging (gradually) upon the space of. Page 42.

**energy:** the capacity of doing work at any instance by a body (a mass) or system of bodies. Title page.

**energy, live:** energy (such as an electrical flow) generated by a being. Page 9.

**energy potential:** in physics, *energy* is defined as the capacity of doing work at any instance by a body (a mass) or system of bodies. *Potential* means possible as opposed to actual. Hence, *energy potential* is the amount of energy something is capable of producing. Thus, *"other producers of electrical flows act on the principle that a difference of energy potential in two or more areas can cause an electrical impulse to flow between or amongst them,"* references two or more sources of energy, one capable of producing more energy than the other, which will cause an electrical flow to occur from the one with greater potential to that one with lesser. This is commonly seen in a battery where one side is indicated as negative (higher potential) and the other positive (lower potential), with the electrical current flowing from negative to positive. Title page.

**entities:** ridges that "think." They form a very complex pattern. They have geographical areas in the body. These areas are standard, preclear to preclear. These areas answer up on an E-Meter like actual minds rather than compartments of a mind. Entities are described in *Scientology: A History of Man.* Page 116.

**enturbulence:** the state or condition of turbulence, agitation or disturbance. Page 97.

**E-therapist:** one who practiced Examiner Therapy, an off-beat, altered technique of setting up a circuit in the mind called "the examiner" and then trying to have this circuit automatically run out engrams. It did not work. Page 117.

**evaluate:** to conclude for or tell a preclear what is wrong with him or what to think about his case. Page 5.

**exclamation points, with:** an exclamation point is a sign (!) used in writing after a statement that shows strong feeling, enthusiasm, wonder, surprise, etc. Using more than one such sign, as in doing something *"with exclamation points"* shows this with even greater intensity. Page 29.

**exhibitionism:** the tendency to call attention to oneself, show off or display. Page 80.

**exudes:** projects or radiates abundantly. Page 109.

**faith:** unquestioning belief or trust. Page 5.

**fall away:** to decay, perish, vanish or become detached and go away. Page 75.

**feeds back:** returns or gives back to as the effect of some process such as the body giving a feeling, awareness or the like about a certain state or condition. Page 67.

**field:** a region, volume or space where a specific, measurable influence, force, etc., exists. Page 30.

**flow:** a transfer of energy from one point to another. Title page.

**formula, Life** $= \frac{EI}{-R} \cdot (-f)$: mathematically the formula states that Life equals Energy Potential multiplied by Energy Flow divided by Negative Resistance multiplied by Negative Frequency. Title page.

**frequency:** the rate of recurrence of any regularly repeated event, such as a vibration; the number of times that such an event occurs in a given unit of time, usually a second. For instance, if a string on a piano vibrated up and down 440 times per second, then its frequency would be 440 times per second. Title page.

**gallantry:** nobility of spirit or action; courage and heroic bravery. Page 41.

**generator:** a machine that converts one form of energy into another, especially mechanical energy into electrical energy. In an electrical generator, the solid iron base of the generator, fastened to a floor or table, imposes time and space upon the two terminals. Without this imposition of time and space, no energy could be possible. A great deal of mechanical motion must be put into an electrical generator because an electrical generator is discharging between the dichotomy of *effort* and *matter.* Page 66.

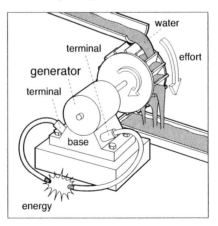

**genetic entity:** the genetic line consists of the total of incidents which have occurred during the evolution of the MEST body itself. The composite of these facsimiles has the semblance of a being.

This being would be called the *genetic entity* or the GE. The genetic entity is fully described in *Scientology: A History of Man*. Page 101.

**genus:** a major subdivision in the classification of organisms. Several closely related species, or one species, make up one genus. Title page.

**Governor, The:** the speed of the preclear. How fast does he run, how fast he can change flows, how much energy he can make. It is an analogy to a *governor,* a mechanical device which controls the speed of an engine. It is used here to mean a sort of speed-control mechanism used by an individual to speed himself up or slow himself down in order to meet various situations in life. One can decide to run fast or slow and the governor puts the theta facsimile of that speed into use, affecting the metabolism and everything else concerned with the body. To run slow it will pick up or postulate or imagine a slow facsimile and then run on it. Or it can postulate a fast theta facsimile and run on it. Further information can be found in the lecture of 24 October 1951, "Being Right." Available in the Research & Discovery volumes. Page 65.

**grim:** (of a fact, truth or the like) possibly difficult, unpleasant or shocking to confront, but used humorously in the text to mean the opposite. Page 17.

**gross:** physically large; bulky. Page 22.

**ground:** to connect to the earth so that electrical charge will flow into the ground. This provides a harmless path to drain off stray or excess electrical currents. Earth conducts electricity, so if an appliance, piece of equipment or any item that is electrically charged is connected to the ground, electrical energy will flow out of the item and into the earth. The human body also conducts electricity, and an electrical charge that is generated in the body will flow out of the body and into the earth if the body is in contact with it. Page 70.

groundings: *see* ground.

hang up: to suspend from a hook or rail. Hence, "hang up in time" refers to suspended in time. Page 10.

hard-boiled: marked by a direct, clearheaded approach; realistic. Page 42.

harmonic: used to describe a frequency (number of vibrations per second) which is a multiple of a "fundamental" frequency. If one stretches a string, or rubber band, and strikes it, a tone or note is produced. One can measure the number of times per second that string is vibrating. Another string, vibrating at certain, but different, multiples of that vibration rate will sound pleasing. This is calculated out mathematically such as 1, 1/2, 1/3, 1/4, etc. Such can be seen with strings in a piano, each one different in length and vibrating at different rates per second. By striking two or more at a time, simultaneously, one can hear which notes are harmonious (pleasing) when played together and which are disharmonious (harsh or not pleasing). Thus, by extension, something which repeats characteristics at a higher or lower point on a scale will be harmonic and seem to be similar and agreeable. Page 41.

harmony: a combination of parts in accord with each other, so as to form a consistent and pleasing whole. The word comes from the field of music where certain combinations of tones sound pleasing to the ear. *See also* disharmony. Page 41.

have nothing (further) to do with: not be associated or involved with something (anymore or any longer); have no (more) dealings with something. Page 115.

heavy facsimile: used to be known as an engram. In view of the fact that it has been found to be stored elsewhere than in the cells, the term *heavy facsimile* has now come into use. A heavy facsimile is an experience, complete with all perceptions and emotions and thoughts and efforts, occupying a precise place in space and a moment in time. It can be an operation, an injury, a term of heavy physical exertion, or even a death. It is composed of the preclear's own effort and the effort of the environment (counter-effort); a heavy facsimile is one containing a great deal of thought, emotion, effort or pain. See *Advanced Procedure and Axioms* and *Electropsychometric Auditing* contained in the *Technique 88: Incidents on the Track Before Earth* lecture series package supplement. Page 11.

**Hegel:** Georg Wilhelm Friedrich Hegel (1770-1831), German philosopher who set forth a philosophical system on the basis that reality can only be understood as a totality ("the truth is the whole"), and that the attempt to understand the apparently individual and unconnected phenomena of nature, history and human life was utterly mistaken. As an example, Hegel claimed that, given the mystic qualities of the number 7, there could only be seven planets around the Sun. So great was Hegel's authority that when Italian astronomer Piazzi (1746-1826) actually observed an eighth planet with his telescope, his discovery was denied and the evidence discarded because it violated Hegel's principles. Page 15.

**holder:** something that holds another thing in place. Page 74.

**holder:** in Dianetics, a *holder* is a type of action phrase (words or phrases in engrams or locks which cause the individual to perform involuntary actions on the time track). A holder holds the preclear at a point on the track. ("Stay here," "Don't leave me," "Hold onto this," "Don't let go," etc.) The subject of holders is described in *Dianetics: The Modern Science of Mental Health*. Page 86.

**honor:** adherence to actions or principles considered right, moral and of high standard; integrity; a fine sense of what is right and wrong. Page 41.

**"*hot* facsimiles":** facsimiles that contain heat. The body moving through facsimiles sometimes hits hot facsimiles. It's heat that can be measured with a thermometer. You start running an enturbulence area, a heavy conflict area, and you generally get heat. A person will feel just like he's burning, like he's on fire. Page 43.

**Hubbard Association of Scientologists:** at the time this book was written, the organization that served as the central dissemination and training center for Dianetics and Scientology. See *Addresses* for current organization locations. Page 119.

**humanities:** the branches of learning concerned with human thought and relations, as distinguished from the sciences; especially language, literature, history and philosophy. Page 15.

**hung up:** halted or snagged. *See also* **hang up**. Page 16.

**I:** an abbreviation for *intensity* and used as an electrical symbol for strength of a current. Title page.

**illusion:** something that deceives the senses or mind, for example, by appearing to exist when it does not or appearing to be one thing when it is in fact another. Page 16.

**implanted:** fixed or instilled deeply an idea, belief, desire, command or the like, in a person's mind or consciousness, as through force, pain, etc. Page 24.

**implode:** to burst inwards, as opposed to explode (outwards). Page 11.

**imposes:** puts or places (something) on or upon; establishes. Page 98.

**impulse:** a single, usually sudden, flow or surge of electrical current in one direction. Page 66.

**index:** a sign or indication of something. Page 9.

**Indian philosophy:** the systems of thought and reflection that were developed by the civilizations of the Indian subcontinent (large region in southern Asia, including the countries of Bangladesh, India and Pakistan). Indian thought has been concerned with various philosophical problems, significant among them the nature of the world, the nature of reality, the nature of knowledge, ethics and religion. The sacred texts of Indian culture and philosophy include the Veda, which contain the Vedic Hymns, the earliest learned writings of which we have any record on Earth. They tell about evolution, about Man coming into this universe and the curve of life which is birth, growth, degenerate and decay. Page 15.

**infinite:** without any limits that can be measured. Page 24.

**infinity (∞):** the condition of being unable to be measured; the state or quality of being infinite, having no limit or end. Page 22.

**inflict:** to give or cause (pain, wounds, etc.) by or as by striking. Page 10.

**in (one's) turn:** in (one's) proper order in a series. Used to express an act that appropriately and naturally follows a similar act done by another. Page 5.

**in other words:** put differently, otherwise stated, often used to introduce an explanation of something and usually in a simpler way. Page 30.

**"in-run":** a reference to a method of processing in which the preclear is asked to get the concept of having a certain feeling, as for example, to run the concept of tiredness. *See also* **"out-run."** Page 47.

**instantaneousness:** the condition of happening immediately or almost immediately. Page 99.

**interaction:** the action or influence of persons or things on each other. Page 10.

**interlocked:** engaged or interrelated with one another; locked into one another. Page 10.

**interplay:** action, effect or influence on each other or one another; interaction. Page 10.

**in the course of:** while doing; during the progress or length of. Page 94.

**Kant:** Immanuel Kant (1724–1804), German philosopher who asserted methods of attaining knowledge based on the principles of transcendentalism (the principles of reality are to be discovered not from experience, but by a study of the processes of thought), and declared that things lying beyond experience such as human freedom, the soul, immortality or God were unknowable. His stress on seeking the absolute hindered scientific progress while his explanation of the "unknowable" discouraged further investigation of the actual beingness and soul of Man. Page 15.

**kinetic:** a thing of motion. Page 9.

**knocking away:** forcing, sending or driving something away as if by means of a blow or striking; forcefully getting rid of something. Page 48.

**lame, the:** persons who are crippled through injury to, or defect in, a limb. Page 15.

**laws of motion:** *see* laws of Newton.

**laws of Newton:** a reference to three laws formulated by English scientist and mathematician Sir Isaac Newton (1642–1727). These laws in brief are: (1) a body at rest remains at rest and a body in motion remains in motion unless acted on by an external force; (2) the motion of a body changes in proportion to the size of the force applied to it; (3) every action produces an equal but opposite reaction. Page 15.

**lay (something) in:** to put (something) in place or in a position. Page 5.

**liable to:** likely to do something, as in *"liable to survive."* Page 10.

**lies:** is found; consists or is based on (usually followed by *in*). Page 85.

**life continuum:** the phenomenon of an individual's tendency to carry on the fears, goals, habits and manifestations of others who have failed, departed or are dead. Life continuum is described in *Handbook for Preclears* and its companion lecture series *Life Continuum.* Page 86.

**Life $= \frac{EI}{-R} \cdot (-f)$:** mathematically the formula states that Life equals Energy Potential multiplied by Energy Flow divided by Negative Resistance multiplied by Negative Frequency. Title page.

**lighter:** having less stress, force, mass or the like than something else. Page 74.

**light facsimiles:** throughout his lifetime, an individual is perceiving and storing facsimiles. Anything he has ever seen or felt or heard is stored. In the main, the pattern of attention units in the facsimile determines its character. When the facsimile contains pain, heavy emotion, heavy effort, it is comprised of tighter and more compact motions or fields, hence, a *heavy facsimile*. Other facsimiles are lighter and may contain smoothly flowing wave patterns, hence, a *light facsimile*. See *Electropsychometric Auditing* contained in the *Technique 88: Incidents on the Track Before Earth* lecture series package supplement. Wavelengths and patterns of energy are further described throughout *Scientology 8-80*. Page 17.

**live energy:** energy (such as an electrical flow) generated by a being. Page 9.

**lock:** an analytical moment in which the perceptics of an engram are approximated, thus restimulating the engram or bringing it into action, the present time perceptics being erroneously interpreted by the reactive mind to mean that the same condition which produced physical pain once before is now again at hand. See *Science of Survival.* Page 29.

**Lock Scanning:** a process in which one contacts an early lock on the track and goes rapidly or slowly through all such similar incidents straight to present time. One does this many times and the whole chain of locks becomes ineffective in influencing one. Lock Scanning is described in *Science of Survival.* Page 29.

**Lorentz-FitzGerald:** a reference to Dutch physicist Hendrik Lorentz (1853-1928) and Irish physicist George FitzGerald (1851-1901) who proposed that a moving body exhibits a contraction or shrinking in the direction of its motion by an amount that depends on how closely it approaches the speed of light. This theory was later used by German-born physicist Albert Einstein (1879-1955), when developing his own theories on the characteristics of matter as its velocity approaches the speed of light. Page 102.

**low-scale concepts:** a reference to the Chart of Attitudes which plots the ideal state of being and one's attitudes and reactions in life. "I Am Not" and "I Know Not" are at the bottom of the chart, 0.5, Apathy. See *Handbook for Preclears.* Page 30.

**magnetism:** the properties of attraction possessed by magnets. Page 15.

**make up (one's) own mind:** decide something for oneself; come to a decision or conclusion about something. Page 29.

**Man:** the human race or species, humankind, Mankind. Page 15.

**man:** a human being, without regard to sex or age; a person. Page 16.

**many a:** noting each one of a large but indefinite number. Page 15.

**matter:** the substance, or the substances collectively, out of which a physical object is made or of which it consists. Page 15.

**maybe:** in any engram there is a "maybe," two choices, which are relatively evenly balanced. Their even balancing makes an irresolution (the condition of wavering in decision, purpose or opinion). The one thing holding up beingness is indecision–a "maybe." The anatomy of maybe is covered in the lecture series *The Route to Infinity*. Page 10.

**mechanical: 1.** from the word *mechanics* which means the procedural or operating details (of something). When applied to theories, *mechanical* means explaining phenomena by the assumption of mechanical action; the explanation of how something works. Page 23.

**2.** done by or involving physical forces. Page 66.

**mechanism:** the agency or means by which an effect is produced or a purpose is accomplished, likened to the structure or system of parts in a mechanical device for carrying out some function or doing something. Page 93.

**mechanisms, control:** means or systems that operate to restrain, regulate or dominate a person, his ideas, emotions, judgment or the like. Page 23.

**MEST Clear:** an individual who no longer retains engrams or locks. Page 30.

**mirror:** that which reflects, represents or acts to copy something. Page 9.

**misreason:** the prefix *mis-* means badly, wrongly, erroneously or mistakenly, usually relating to the manner in which something is carried out. *Reason* includes logical, rational and analytical thought and *misreason* thus includes thought which is illogical, irrational, not analytical and erroneous. Page 24.

**mistake any of (one's) moves:** act in an erroneous way concerning any of the actions one takes to accomplish something. Page 29.

**mockery:** an imitation, especially of a ridiculous or unsatisfactory kind. Page 73.

**mock-up:** something which exists in present time and sits someplace. It is not in the past. It is right here. It is made by the preclear. Page 73.

**motivator:** a motivator is an incident which happens to the preclear and which he dramatizes. Page 56.

**motor:** of, pertaining to or involving muscular movement. Page 117.

**moves, mistake any of (one's):** act in an erroneous way concerning any of the actions one takes to accomplish something. Page 29.

**mystic:** baffling or incomprehensible to the understanding; pertaining to mysterious qualities, from the idea that mysticism involves religious or spiritual powers that most people don't or can't understand. Page 100.

**negative:** something that is opposite in direction, position, quality, etc., from something (arbitrarily) designated positive. Title page.

**negative command:** ask the preclear *not* to be a foot back of his head. Give him commands in the negative which will be obeyed in the positive sense. Page 116.

**negative positive:** a reference to the dual polarity of any terminal where there is an alternating current flow. In standard electrical textbooks, a positive (plus) terminal and a negative (minus) terminal are required to create an electrical flow. In an alternating current, the electrical energy flows first in one direction from terminal A to terminal B and then reverses and flows from terminal B to terminal A, then A to B, etc., back and forth many times per second. In order for an alternating current to flow in both directions, each terminal must have a dual polarity–thus the positive terminal would need to be both positive and positive negative and the negative terminal both negative and negative positive, thus resulting in four terminals: positive and positive negative, negative and negative positive. For the relationship to auditing, see Chapter Seventeen. Page 98.

**Newton, laws of:** a reference to three laws formulated by English scientist and mathematician Sir Isaac Newton (1642-1727). These laws in brief are: (1) a body at rest remains at rest and a body in motion remains in motion unless acted on by an external force; (2) the motion of a body changes in proportion to the size of the force applied to it; (3) every action produces an equal but opposite reaction. Page 15.

Nietzsche: Friedrich Wilhelm Nietzsche (1844-1900), German philosopher and poet. In his book *Thus Spake Zarathustra,* Nietzsche presents as a desirable code of conduct unlimited willingness to destroy. This laid in the doctrine for the superrace envisioned by Adolf Hitler and the Nazi regime which held as an ideal unlimited creation and destruction. Page 15.

not-beingness: the state of being an effect, being effected by some exterior cause. Page 30.

nuclear physics: the branch of physics that deals with the behavior, structure and component parts of the center of an atom (called the nucleus), which constitutes almost all of the mass of the atom. Page 10.

null, void: a reference to the phrase *null and void,* meaning of no value, consequence or effect. Page 30.

obsess: to fill the mind of; keep the attention of to an unreasonable or unhealthy extent; haunt. Page 24.

obsessed: having an obsession (the domination of one's thoughts or feelings by a persistent idea, image, desire, etc.). Page 24.

obsessive: pertaining to or resembling an obsession (the domination of one's thoughts or feelings by a persistent idea, image, desire, etc.); besieged by. Page 24.

occluded: affected by *occlusion,* i.e., having memories shut off from one's awareness; from *occlude,* to close, shut or stop up (a passage, opening, etc.). Page 69.

occlusions: hidden areas or incidents on the time track. Page 25.

1, 2, 3 processes: processes which are easy to run, following an exact procedure with individual steps (i.e., 1, 2, 3). Page 29.

**on the other hand:** used to indicate two contrasting sides of a subject; in contrast, oppositely. Page 100.

**operative:** being in effect; having force or influence; operating. Page 15.

**opportunely:** rightly or fitting; appropriately and advantageously for the purpose. Page 116.

**oscilloscopes:** electronic instruments that display changing electrical signals. The signals appear as wavy lines or in other patterns on a screen. Page 100.

**other than, be:** (usually used in negative statements) be different than something else. Page 30.

**out of: 1.** literally, from a position within to the outside of. Hence, to rid of from some specified place, condition, etc., as in *"get the facsimiles out of present time."* Page 16.

**2.** in a state or position away from the expected or usual, as in *"enough force to bow his back out of shape."* Page 23.

**3.** because of; owing to, as in *"Out of an obsessive aberration, all beauty becomes hideous."* Page 24.

**4.** from within to the outside of, as in *"consists of getting the thetan out of the body immediately."* Page 115.

**"out-run":** a reference to a method of processing in which the preclear is asked to get the concept of making someone else have a certain feeling, as for example, to run the concept of making somebody else tired. *See also* **"in-run."** Page 47.

**overt:** an overt act (which may also be covert or accidental) is an incident which the preclear does to another dynamic. Page 56.

**parentheses (-f):** both of a pair of the upright curved lines ( ) used in a mathematical expression to sometimes mark off a number or quantity that is to be multiplied by another number or quantity. For example, in multiplying 3 times 3 one can write either 3 • 3 or

(3) • (3). The dot between the two 3s is a symbol for multiplication. Title page.

**partake of:** to share the nature of; to have some of the qualities or characteristics of. Page 15.

**pattern:** an arrangement of form; disposition of parts or elements. Page 9.

**perishable:** something liable to decay or die. Page 30.

**perpetuate:** to cause to endure or continue indefinitely; to preserve from extinction or oblivion. Page 103.

**personalness:** the quality of being personal; having the characteristic or nature of a person or a rational, self-conscious being, as opposed to a thing. Page 30.

**pervade:** to pass or spread throughout all parts. Page 17.

**philosophies:** systems of thought concerning the larger issues and deeper meanings in life and events. Page 15.

**picking up:** looking for and selecting something, as for the purpose of dealing with it. Page 119.

**pick up:** to take hold of. Page 118.

**play, come into:** come into operation or motion; become active or in force. Page 56.

**played:** 1. caused to move or pass on or over; struck lightly upon something, as in *"played lightly over a facsimile."* Page 11.
2. operated continuously or with repeated action, as in *"live units are played on it."* Page 17.

**played against:** literally, aimed or directed at, sometimes continuously, as in *"played against motion."* Page 9.

**plus negative:** a reference to the dual polarity of any terminal where there is an alternating current flow. In standard electrical textbooks, a positive (plus) terminal and a negative (minus) terminal are required to create an electrical flow. In an alternating current, the electrical energy flows first in one direction from terminal A to terminal B and then reverses and flows from terminal B to terminal A, then A to B, etc., back and forth many times per second. In order for an alternating current to flow in both directions, each terminal must have a dual polarity–thus the positive terminal would need to be both positive and positive negative and the negative terminal both negative and negative positive, thus resulting in four terminals: positive and positive negative, negative and negative positive. For the relationship to auditing, see Chapter Seventeen. Page 98.

**point out:** indicate or direct somebody's attention to something. Page 74.

**postulates:** conclusions, decisions or resolutions made by the individual himself on his own self-determinism on data of the past known or unknown. The postulate is always known. It is made upon the evaluation of data by the individual or on impulse without data. It resolves a problem of the past, decides on problems or observations in the present or sets a pattern for the future. The subject of postulates is described in *Advanced Procedure and Axioms*. Page 36.

**potential:** possible, as opposed to actual. Thus *energy potential* is the amount of power something is capable of producing. *See also* **energy potential**. Title page.

**predominate(s):** to be of or have greater quantity or number. Page 69.

**pressor:** *see* **pressor beam**.

**pressor beam:** a beam which can be put out by a thetan which acts as a stick and with which one can thrust oneself away or thrust things away. The pressor beam can be lengthened and, in lengthening, pushes away. Pressor beams are used to direct action. Page 66.

**propitiation:** the action of making someone favorably inclined or preventing someone from being angry or impatient by doing something to please them. Page 52.

**proton:** a tiny particle of matter that has a positive electrical charge. Page 98.

**proximity:** the fact, condition or position of being near or close in space. Page 66.

**purity:** the quality or condition of being pure; specifically, freedom from evil, sin or moral fault or other impure elements or qualities. Page 41.

**randomity:** the misalignment through the internal or external efforts by other forms of life or the material universe of the efforts of an organism, and is imposed on the physical organism by counter-efforts in the environment. A description of randomity and all its manifestations is contained in the Dianetic Axioms. See *Advanced Procedure and Axioms*. Page 101.

**ranges:** moves or passes, as if by traveling along or through an area. Page 99.

**"read":** to observe and note the movements of something, such as a needle on a meter, and to understand the information conveyed by these movements. Page 36.

**reducing:** rendering free of aberrative material as far as possible. Page 17.

**resistance:** the quantity of opposition of a body or substance to the flow of energy passing through it. Title page.

**resounding:** expressed in a rich, full or impressive manner. Used sarcastically. Page 15.

**retractor wave:** it is possible for a wave to act as a *retractor*. That is to say, it is possible for certain waves to pull back instead of push out. You turn a hose on somebody. This pushes him back. There can exist a wave which, if it were a hose, would pull you up to the nozzle instead of pushing you away. Thetans can put out such a retractor wave. You have to hang together a solid flow, so to speak, and then make the solid flow collapse in order to get a retractor wave. It's to grab hold of something and hold it and pull it in. Also called *retractor beam* and *tractor beam*. Page 55.

**rickety:** liable to fall or break down because of being weak; shaky. Page 67.

**ridden to death:** oppressed to an excessive degree (likened to a horse being sat on and managed by a dominating rider). *Death* in this sense means to an intolerable degree; extremely. Page 15.

**riddle:** something that is difficult to understand or presents a problem that needs to be solved. Page 15.

**ridge:** an area of dense waves. A ridge is caused by two energy flows coinciding and causing an enturbulence of energy which on examination is found to take on a characteristic which–in energy flows–is very like matter, having its particles in chaotic mixture. Page 51.

**run out:** to exhaust the negative influence of something; to erase. Page 17.

**salvo:** a simultaneous or successive discharge of artillery, bombs, etc. Page 81.

**say nothing of, to:** used to introduce a further fact or thing in addition to that already mentioned, and so strengthen the previous statement. Page 23.

**scanned:** glanced over systematically by something, as in *"scanned by live units."* Page 17.

**scan out:** glance over something systematically and remove it from a place or position, as in *"scan out the small action of moving out of the body."* *Out* in this sense, as in *scan out,* means removed from a place, position or situation. Page 116.

174

**Schopenhauer:** Arthur Schopenhauer (1788-1860), German philosopher known for his philosophy of pessimism (tendency to see only the negative or worst aspects of things and expecting mainly bad things to happen) and who believed that only the stopping of desire can solve the universal impulse of the will to live. Page 15.

**scores:** a great many. From the word *score,* meaning twenty. Page 48.

**secondaries:** moments of acute loss as death of a loved one. The subject of secondaries and their processing is contained in *Science of Survival.* Page 29.

**secondaries, running of:** a reference to processing addressed to handling secondaries. The text refers to auditing techniques contained in *Science of Survival.* Page 29.

**self-perpetuating:** having the power to renew and thus continue itself for an indefinite length of time. Page 103.

**shows up:** appears or is present (in); becomes visible. Page 59.

**shun:** avoid, keep clear of. Page 42.

**sight:** observe or look at something. Page 86.

**single incident running:** also called *single incident processing,* Dianetic auditing that addresses a single incident, such as an engram, as different from Concept Running where the preclear addresses many incidents in response to an auditing command. See *Dianetics: The Modern Science of Mental Health.* Page 29.

**slipping off:** passing or going off or away from the proper or desired position, as if with a sliding motion. Page 35.

**somatics:** physical pains, discomforts, etc. Page 30.

**some little time:** *some* is used here to mean not little, a large number or amount of something. *Little* also can be used with an opposite meaning. Hence, the entire phrase means a lot of time. Page 69.

**spares:** saves or relieves someone from experiencing something. Page 35.

**spectrum:** the whole range of something, such as the colors of light, each color having its own wavelength. Page 100.

**spotty:** having or marked with uneven patches or spots; not uniformly all of one color, shade or the like. Page 35.

**state of affairs:** the way in which conditions, situations, events or circumstances stand within a particular sphere or at a particular time. Page 79.

**static:** pertaining to or characterized by a fixed or stationary condition, lacking movement or motion. Page 10.

**"sticky":** 1. lacking free and smooth movement or progress; resistant to change; impeded, as in *"If the needle stops or is 'sticky.'"* Page 36.

2. having the quality of adhering to something or of holding on to something as if by means of glue, as in *"form a base 'sticky' enough."* Page 37.

**Straightwire:** the name of a process. It is the act of stringing a line between present time and some incident in the past, and stringing that line directly and without any detours. The auditor is stringing a straight "wire" of memory between the actual genus (origin) of a condition and present time, thus demonstrating that there is a difference of time and space in the condition then and the condition now, and that the preclear, conceding this difference, then rids himself of the condition or at least is able to handle it. See *Self Analysis.* Page 29.

**strip away:** take away. *Away* in this sense means to remove, separate or eliminate. Page 17.

**stuff, sturdier:** stronger, firmer and more determined in basic qualities or inward character (stuff). Page 23.

**summed:** described concisely. Page 30.

**sweep over (something):** pass along or across something as if with a rapid, steady, continuous motion. Page 23.

**take on:** to assume or acquire as or as if one's own. Page 97.

**take (something) off:** to remove, as in *"If we had to take the emotion, effort and reason or misreason off the whole track, we would have a long task."* Page 24.

**take (something) on faith:** to accept or believe (something) on the basis of little or no evidence. Hence, *"take very little on faith"* means that something is quite evident based on facts. Page 5.

**takes over:** assumes the control or possession of. Page 110.

**terminal:** a conductor (something which allows electricity to flow) attached at the point where electricity enters and/or leaves a circuit; for example, on a battery there is a terminal at either end. Page 98.

**that is to say:** a phrase used to introduce a clearer, more comprehensible restatement of what immediately precedes or to limit or modify it. Page 42.

**the better to \_\_\_\_:** so as to do the specified thing more effectively. Page 43.

**theta being:** the preclear himself, the "I". Page 17.

**Theta Clear:** a person who can get in and out of his body at will. Page 59.

**time, some little:** *some* is used here to mean not little, a large number or amount of something. *Little* also can be used with an opposite meaning. Hence, the entire phrase means a lot of time. Page 69.

**Tone Scale:** a scale of emotional tones which shows the levels of human behavior. These tones, ranged from the highest to the lowest, are in part, Enthusiasm, Conservatism, Boredom, Antagonism, Anger, Covert Hostility, Fear, Grief and Apathy. Page 82.

177

**to say nothing of:** used to introduce a further fact or thing in addition to that already mentioned, and so strengthen the previous statement. Page 23.

**tractor beams:** beams put out by a thetan in order to pull things toward him. The tractor beam is an energy flow which the thetan shortens. If one placed a flashlight beam upon a wall and then, by manipulating the beam, brought the wall closer to him by it, he would have the action of a tractor beam. Also called *retractor beam* and *retractor wave.* Page 66.

**tractor-pressor combination:** *see* **tractor beams** and **pressor beam.** Tractors and pressors commonly exist together with the tractor as a loop outside the pressor. The two together stabilize one another. Page 74.

**try one's wits:** to subject one's mental faculties, powers or senses to severe test or strain. Page 29.

**tumble into view:** appear or become visible, as if rolling or spilling out. Page 47.

**turn back time:** a variation of *turn back the clock,* go back in time. Hence, to restore past conditions or reverse some change. Page 10.

**turn upon:** to aim, focus or direct (something) on. Page 11.

**Valence Shifting:** auditing that shifts the preclear out of the valence of others and into his own valence. The text refers to the processing contained in *Handbook for Preclears.* Page 29.

**Veda, the:** the Vedic Hymns, the earliest recorded learned writings. They are the most ancient sacred literature of the Hindus (the natives of India) comprising over a hundred books still in existence. They tell about evolution, about Man coming into this universe and the curve of life, which is birth, growth, degenerate and decay.

**veneer:** an attractive appearance that covers or disguises someone or something's true nature or feelings. From a thin decorative or outward covering of fine wood applied to a coarser wood or other material. Page 94.

**vibration:** a continuous, rhythmic movement back and forth. Page 69.

**visio:** a visible recall, such as a picture or scene which has been recalled by seeing it again. Page 51.

**wavelength:** a wavelength is the distance from the peak (crest) to the peak (crest) of a wave. Wavelength is described in Chapter Four. Page 9.

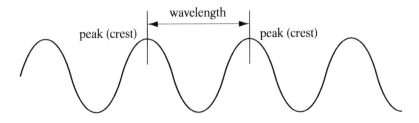

**well:** proper or right, appropriate. Page 70.

**which is to say:** a phrase used to introduce a clearer, more comprehensible restatement of what immediately precedes or to limit or modify it. Page 99.

**while (the):** at the same time. Page 47.

**wholesale:** on a large scale. Page 29.

**whole track:** the entire track of a theta being beyond (earlier than) the present life. The subject of whole track is contained in *Scientology: A History of Man* and its companion lecture series *Technique 88: Incidents on the Track Before Earth.* Page 24.

**will, do what (one):** used to mean that whatever one does, it doesn't matter because the condition or result will be the same. Page 65.

**-wise:** *(informal)* a word ending used to mean concerning or related to a particular thing, as in *"mirror-wise."* Page 15.

**with exclamation points:** an exclamation point is a sign (!) used in writing after a statement that shows strong feeling, enthusiasm, wonder, surprise, etc. Using more than one such sign, as in doing something *"with exclamation points"* shows this with even greater intensity. Page 29.

**within the bounds of:** inside the boundaries of something, as if lying within a particular region or sphere of activity that is marked or set apart from others. Page 102.

**w.l.:** abbreviation for *wavelength*. Page 22.

**worked:** acted upon or influenced, as with a technique. Page 67.

# $\mathcal{I}$NDEX

decreasing control
distance, 52

patterns of attention or wave
flows, 55

ridges from past bodies, 51
Tone Scale of
Wavelengths, 22

wave, 21

**dichotomies**, 65, 68-70, 80-82

basic, 73

most important, 75

running Sub-zero Scale
as, 116

try to prevent from using, 75

use of, 69

**difference of potential**

creation of energy by, 66, 67

**direct current**, 67

**disagree**

see **Agree-Disagree**

**disagreement**, 69, 74

**"Disbelief,"** 30

**discharge**, 99, 110

backwards, 102

discharging condenser, 66,
100

wave characteristic and, 100

**disharmony**

of wave motion, 41

theta and, 42

**dispersal**, 55

definition, 97

of thetan through ridges, 110

reverse, 97

**"Distrust,"** 30

**dub-in**, 111

**dynamics**

Cause on eight, 74

# E

**effort**, 9, 24, 36, 67, 102, 118

dichotomies, 68, 75, 99

**Effort–Apathy**, 68

**Effort Processing**, 29

**8-80**, 87

**elasticity**

flow, 102

**electrical current**

generation of, 67

preclear and, 30

**electrical field**, 10

**electrical flow**, 66

**electrical generator**, 66

imposition of time and space
by, 98

**electrical shocks**

facsimile and, 23

**electricity**

error, 98

description, 97
facsimiles in body and, 116
from past bodies, diagram, 51
seem able to think, 119
thetan's own energy in, 119
used by life source, 100

**Right-Wrong**, 68

# S

**sadness**
of bodies dying, 118

**Sane-Insane**, 68

**sanity**
dwindling, what it is, 99
enhancement of, 103
semblance of, 91

**Schopenhauer**, 15

**Scientology**
basic to nuclear physics, 10
minor goal of, 11

*Scientology: A History of Man*, 29, 30, 82

**screen**
description, 97

**secondaries**
running of, 29

**Second Dynamic**, 74

**self-determinism**, 73-75
definition, 99

most important step in
establishing a preclear's, 65
rehabilitate preclear's, 5
Technique 8-80, 115
total components of, 99
whiteness, 73

**Serenity of beingness**, 92

**sex**
wave just below beauty, 56

**sight**, 9, 118

**single incident processing**, 29

**skull**, 110

**slavery**
electronic implants and, 30

**"slowness"**
body and, 67

**solidity**, 67

**somatics**, 30
ridges and, 119
transfer of, 86

**sound**, 9

**space**
laws of
thought, behavior and, 15

**speed**, 99
potential and, 99
production of energy, 65
sufficient output to overcome
facsimiles, 17

**Start-Stop**, 68